J B Fra
Warrick, Karen Clemens.
Benjamin Franklin :
creating a nation

$20.95
ocm51726854

WITHDRAWN

Karen Clemens Warrick

Enslow Publishers, Inc.

40 Industrial Road
Box 398
Berkeley Heights, NJ 07922
USA

PO Box 38
Aldershot
Hants GU12 6BP
UK

http://www.enslow.com

Copyright © 2004 by Karen Clemens Warrick

All rights reserved.

No part of this book may be reproduced by any means
without the written permission of the publisher.

Library of Congress Cataloging-in-Publication Data

Warrick, Karen Clemens.
Benjamin Franklin : creating a nation / Karen Clemens Warrick.
p. cm. — (America's founding fathers)
Includes bibliographical references and index.
ISBN 0-7660-2195-5
1. Franklin, Benjamin, 1706-1790—Juvenile literature.
2. Statesmen—United States—Biography—Juvenile literature.
3. Scientists—United States—Biography—Juvenile literature.
4. Inventors—United States—Biography—Juvenile literature.
5. Printers—United States—Biography—Juvenile literature. [1. Franklin, Benjamin, 1706-1790. 2. Statesmen. 3. Inventors.] I. Title. II. Series.
E302.6.F8W28 2003
973.3'092—dc21

2003002272

Printed in the United States of America

10 9 8 7 6 5 4 3 2 1

To Our Readers: We have done our best to make sure all Internet Addresses in this book were active and appropriate when we went to press. However, the author and the publisher have no control over and assume no liability for the material available on those Internet sites or on other Web sites they may link to. Any comments or suggestions can be sent by e-mail to comments@enslow.com or to the address on the back cover.

Illustration Credits: Charles Penniman, Philadelphia, Pennsylvania, p. 44; CIGNA Museum and Art Collection, p. 38; Dictionary of American Portraits, published by Dover Publications, Inc., in 1967, p. 66; Enslow Publishers, Inc., pp. 27, 70; June Ponte, p. 1; Library of Congress, pp. 14, 21, 31, 32, 34, 36, 43, 47, 50, 54, 74, 80, 81, 87, 94, 101, 103, 111, 115; National Archives, pp. 2–3, 4–5, 9, 59, 78, 88, 91, 106, 116–117.

Cover Illustration: Corel Corporation (background); June Ponte (portrait).

Contents

In the 1770s, many Americans rebelled when England passed laws requiring them to pay new taxes. Here, colonists are depicted attacking a tax collector.

Road to Revolution

BY 1773, TENSION WAS growing between the thirteen American colonies and England, their mother country. Benjamin Franklin was well aware of the problems. He had been a colonial agent in London for the last ten years. He worked for the colonies of Pennsylvania, Massachusetts, New Jersey, and Georgia. It was his job to discuss colonial concerns with British government officials. He worked hard to find solutions.

Franklin's home was located in Philadelphia, Pennsylvania, but he saw himself as a loyal British citizen. He accepted the fact that all colonists were expected to obey laws passed by Parliament, Great Britain's governing body. Most Americans agreed with him. However, the colonies were used to making and obeying some of their own laws. They resisted when King George III and Parliament passed laws requiring the colonists to pay new taxes. They had no representation in Parliament. They claimed that taxation without representation was unfair.

Taxation without Representation

The French and Indian War was fought between England and France from 1754 to 1763. This war left England with big bills to pay. British troops had defended the colonies during the war. Britain thought that Americans should help pay those bills.

In the 1760s, Parliament began to levy taxes, or special fees. One of these taxes, called the Stamp Act, made it necessary to buy a British stamp for every piece of printed paper used. The stamps proved that the tax had been paid. They were needed on all official documents, licenses, and even playing cards. A stamp for a college degree cost two pounds. A liquor license stamp cost four pounds. A stamp for a pack of cards required one shilling (twelve pennies). An almanac stamp cost two pence (two pennies).

The act angered colonists, who thought of themselves as British citizens. British citizens had the right to vote on their own taxes. Colonists expected the same right. But no one represented them in Parliament, and they complained that they were being taxed without representation. Franklin testified before Parliament and helped get the Stamp Act repealed.

The Boston Tea Party

For the most part, the colonists avoided paying Parliament's taxes until the spring of 1773. Then Parliament put a tax on tea shipped to the colonies. Almost all colonists drank tea. They rebelled when the beverage was taxed.

In Boston on December 16, 1773, one hundred fifty colonists disguised themselves as Mohawk Indians. They crept aboard a ship in the harbor loaded with tea from England. The group of men, called the Sons of Liberty, dumped 10,000 pounds of British tea overboard to protest the tax.

Franklin was upset when news of the Boston Tea Party (the name by which the event became known) reached England. He considered it "an act of violent injustice."[1] He wrote and advised the Massachusetts Assembly—the colony's legislature—to pay for the destroyed tea as quickly as possible.

Meanwhile, Parliament decided to teach Boston a lesson. They closed Boston Harbor. No ships were allowed to sail in or out until the city paid for the destroyed tea. This stopped trade, hurting the city's merchants and the shipowners' businesses.

When the people of Boston still refused to pay, Parliament passed laws banning Massachusetts's town meetings and the election of officials. The king also appointed an army general, Lieutenant General Thomas Gage, as the new governor of the colony. The colonists called these laws the Intolerable Acts. Franklin finally offered to pay for the tea himself if these laws were removed. But Great Britain's Parliament refused to negotiate.

Great Britain began to treat the colonists more like subjects instead of citizens with equal rights.[2] No one regretted that more than Franklin did. For the first time, he questioned whether Great Britain and the thirteen colonies could reach a peaceful compromise.

Franklin Takes Action

In December 1772 while he was living in London, Franklin acquired a packet of ten letters. Thomas Hutchinson, royal governor of Massachusetts, had written them. Franklin refused to reveal his source and to this day nobody knows how he got the letters.

In the letters, Governor Hutchinson said that the colonists had too much freedom. He wrote, "There must be an abridgement [decrease] of what are called English liberties."[3] He recommended more British troops be sent to the colonies.

Franklin was furious. How could Hutchinson suggest that Englishmen living in America should not have the same rights as those living in the mother country?[4] He believed that colonial leaders needed to know what the governor had written. Franklin sent the letters to the speaker of the house for the Massachusetts Assembly. He thought that the letters would show that misunderstandings had

In 1773, American colonists dumped 10,000 pounds of British tea into Boston Harbor, while disguised as Mohawk Indians.

caused many of the problems with Parliament. He still hoped that communication could be improved and a compromise could be reached through reasonable and peaceful discussions.

Franklin sent special instructions with the letters. He wanted them shown to the colonial leaders, but not copied or printed. Then he wanted the packet returned. These instructions were not followed. (Franklin may have suspected his instructions would be ignored. He said later that he would have published them himself, but had promised not to.)[5]

However, the reaction of the Massachusetts Assembly did not make things better. After reading the letters, the Assembly members wrote a petition. They asked that Hutchinson be removed from his position as colonial governor. This petition was sent to Agent Franklin in London to present to the Privy Council and King George. Then members asked that copies of the letter be printed for their use.

The letters were also published in the *Boston Gazette*. Copies quickly spread throughout the colony. The contents created so much hostility that Hutchinson felt his life was in danger. He fled to England.

In England, the publication of the letters caused more trouble. Parliament wanted to know who had sent these "private letters" to the Massachusetts Assembly. The man to whom the letters had been addressed was dead. His brother, William Whately, swore that no family member was responsible. Instead, Whately accused John Temple, an American living in England, of stealing the letters. To defend his honor, Temple challenged Whately to a duel with swords. After being wounded, Whately gave up the fight.

Franklin was upset when he learned that "two gentlemen . . . unfortunately engaged in a duel about a transaction [matter] . . . of which both of them [were] totally ignorant and innocent."[6] He immediately sent a letter to the newspapers saying he was responsible. He also explained why he had sent the letters to the colonial assembly. Franklin believed that Americans should know who had made these suggestions. It had been Hutchinson, a man born in Massachusetts, who wanted their rights limited and additional troops stationed in the colonies. After learning this, Franklin thought that colonists would be angry with the governor, not Parliament.

Franklin's reasons did little to soothe Parliament's hostile reaction. They held him responsible for the letters' publication. And official opinion did not improve when Franklin presented the Massachusetts petition asking that Hutchinson be removed.

The Privy Council

On January 29, 1774, Franklin was called before Great Britain's Privy Council. He had been told that the council planned to discuss the petition asking for Governor Hutchinson's removal. But it was soon clear that something more was to take place.

The meeting was held in a room called the Cockpit. (The room was named for a rooster-fighting arena located on the site during the reign of Henry VIII.) When Franklin entered the Cockpit, Lord President Earl Gower and thirty-four council members were seated at a table. Solicitor General Alexander Wedderburn, the council's lawyer, stood behind the members. People who wanted to listen filled every corner of the room and overflowed into the hallway. The crowd included a few of Franklin's friends.

The hearing began with a reading of the Massachusetts petition. Then Franklin's lawyer, John Dunning, made a statement. He pointed out that the petition was a political issue. He suggested that a hearing with both parties represented by lawyers was not necessary. (This was Franklin's position.) Unfortunately, Dunning had a lung illness. His voice was so weak that he could not be heard by the audience or even by many of the council members.

Before Dunning finished his statement, Wedderburn interrupted. He began by summarizing the history of the Massachusetts colony. He started with the Stamp Act riots and ended with the threats against Governor Hutchinson's life that had forced him to flee to England. Wedderburn defended Hutchinson's conduct against the Assembly. He said that "his [Hutchinson's] conduct was praiseworthy to a high degree, he had been moderate, patient, and patriotic."[7]

Then he turned his attention to Franklin. Wedderburn stated that this entire misunderstanding "was caused by Dr. Franklin's interference; that the letters were . . . private letters; that they must have been stolen by Dr. Franklin whose . . . motive was to become governor of Massachusetts."[8]

Wedderburn's accusations went on for nearly an hour. "Nothing will acquit Franklin of the charge of obtaining the letters by fraudulent or corrupt means for the most malignant [evil] purposes . . . I hope, my lords that you will mark and brand the man for the honor of this country, of Europe, and of mankind."[9]

One of Franklin's supporters later said that the speech was "so poisonous and vile that many in the audience were deeply embarrassed."[10]

Though Franklin felt that he was falsely accused, he silently stood through the entire ordeal. This was the English custom for anyone being questioned. He did not attempt to answer Wedderburn or to defend himself. His face remained expressionless. His body never moved.

When the hearing ended, Franklin walked out calmly, even though he was furious.[11] By the next morning, he had decided that sending the Hutchinson letters to Boston was "one of the best actions of his life, and . . . he should certainly do [it] again in the same circumstances."[12]

Franklin had reached a new understanding of the situation. He realized that there was no turning back. At that moment, when only a few leaders in America dreamed of independence, Franklin understood that America was headed down the road to revolution.[13]

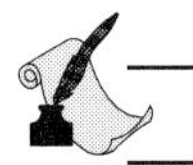

In January 1774, Benjamin Franklin was called before England's Privy Council, where he was accused of stealing letters to tarnish the reputation of Massachusetts Governor Thomas Hutchinson.

The Final Parting

Two days after he appeared before the Privy Council, Franklin was dismissed from his office of Colonial Postmaster General. It was another way to punish him for sending Hutchinson's letters to the colonies.

Franklin's enemies in England spoke out against him. Lord Sandwich called him "one of the bitterest and most mischievous Enemies this Country ever had known."[14] The British press called him "the old veteran of Mischief . . . this old snake."[15]

Meanwhile, his enemies in America voiced their own concerns. As colonial agent, Franklin had always relied on reason and compromise to solve problems between the colonies and Parliament.

Franklin's enemies in America believed that he had been too easy-going about England's mistreatment of the colonies. They thought that he really wanted to win a higher post in the British government.

By October, Franklin was being warned by some of his friends to flee England. They feared that he would be arrested and imprisoned, but he was reluctant to leave. Franklin thought he still might be needed in England. He knew that the colonists had formed the First Continental Congress in September 1774. The delegates wanted to limit Parliament's power over the colonies. They were preparing a petition to the king asking for fair and equal treatment, not independence.

By February 1775, however, Franklin finally decided that he had been away from home too long. He knew that he had done what he could to prevent trouble between Great Britain and the colonies. With no regrets, the elderly patriot sailed for home—to the country where he had been born almost seventy years earlier.

Benjamin Franklin returned home to become one of the most important men in the history of our country—one of our founding fathers. These men dedicated their lives to the idea of an independent nation. Through careful planning, compromise, and hard work, the founding fathers laid a lasting foundation for the United States of America.

Boyhood Years

BENJAMIN FRANKLIN WAS born in Boston on January 17, 1706. This Massachusetts city was the largest seaport in the English colonies. As a young child, he often ran down to the harbor to watch the tall-masted ships sailing in and out. Some of these ships were filled with silks and spices from China or India. Other boats brought slaves from Africa. Benjamin watched as sailors unloaded rum and molasses from the West Indies and goods from Great Britain. All the activity of the busy harbor made him dream of being a sailor when he grew up.[1]

The Franklin Family

Josiah Franklin, Benjamin's father, moved from England to the Massachusetts colony in 1683. He took his first wife, Anne, and their three children with him. He moved because the church his family attended, the Church of England, was becoming more like the Catholic Church. Josiah did not like these changes, but believed it was not safe to speak out against them.

The Franklin family settled in Boston. Josiah looked for work as a dyer. He had practiced the trade of adding color to cloth in England. He soon discovered that Boston already had too many dyers. He needed to find a new trade. Josiah decided to become a chandler, someone who makes soap and candles. He worked very hard at his new business, and so did his children when they were old enough. Many hands were needed to make enough soap and candles to support the Franklin family.

Anne died in 1689 while giving birth to their seventh child. Six months later, Josiah married Abiah Folger, a woman he met at church. Josiah was thirty-two years old. Abiah was ten years younger. Together, they had ten children. Benjamin—Abiah's eighth child and his father's fifteenth—was born in a small house on Milk Street. Because he was one of the youngest children, Benjamin learned to rely on his wits instead of his fists to get along with his older brothers and sisters.

School Years

Benjamin loved books and later said, "I do not remember when I could not read."[2] Josiah realized that his son was bright and decided that he should study for the ministry. When he was eight years old, Benjamin was enrolled in the Boston Latin School. Though the work was hard and the teachers were strict, he did exceptionally well. He was soon at the top of his class.

After Benjamin's first year in school, Josiah decided that he could not afford to pay for his son to become a minister. The Latin School was expensive, and Harvard College, where most students of ministry studied, cost even more. The following year, he sent his son to a less expensive school. At the new school, Benjamin enjoyed his writing lessons, but failed math. His father was very disappointed. He had hoped that Benjamin would learn to keep the books for his business. He decided that it was time Benjamin learned to be a candle and soap maker, and Josiah took his ten-year-old son out of school.

For the next two years, Benjamin worked in his father's shop. He learned to shape wicks. He stirred the smoking vats of tallow (animal fat used to make candles). He worked twelve to fourteen hours each day, six days a week. It was a boring job. Benjamin, a bright, curious boy, hated the routine. He slipped away to Boston Harbor or out to the salt marshes to fish or trap whenever he could.

Josiah soon realized that candle making was not the right trade for his son. He tried to help Benjamin find a trade he liked. He took the boy around Boston to see craftsmen at work. They watched bricklayers, carpenters, and roofers. They studied joiners, who added trim around doors and windows, and braziers, who worked with brass. Josiah wanted to make sure that Benjamin did not follow his childhood dream of running away to sea.

Printer's Apprentice

Twelve-year-old Benjamin finally decided to go to work as a printer's apprentice, or helper. His older brother, James Franklin, had recently opened a print shop in Boston. Benjamin agreed to work for his brother for nine years. He was not happy about the length of time, but soon discovered that he enjoyed the printing business. He liked the smell of printer's ink better than candle tallow. He enjoyed listening to the thump of the wooden press and the crackle of paper while he worked.[3]

Once he started his apprenticeship, Benjamin learned quickly. He worked hard at his job and grew strong. Before long, he could carry a large frame filled with type in each hand as he ran up and down stairs. Other apprentices could carry only half that load.

Working in the printing business also gave Benjamin more chances to read. He became friends with the town bookseller's apprentices that came into the shop. One of them let Benjamin borrow books to read. Another customer shared books with Benjamin from his family's library. And when he had enough money, the young apprentice bought books of his own. Benjamin later said, "Often I sat in my room reading the greatest part of the night, when the book was borrowed in the evening and [had] to be returned early in the morning, lest it should be missed or wanted."[4]

Printing Trade in the 1700s

The printing process in colonial days involved many steps. Apprentices worked for years to master both the physical and mental skills needed. It was the printer's job to set handwritten text in type. A printer placed cast-metal letters in rows to create the lines of printed text. Line after line of text was set in frames. Usually, four pages of type were arranged in one frame. Then the metal letters were coated with ink. Paper was laid over the inked type and pressed against it. Finally, the printed sheet was pulled free and set aside to dry. When all the sheets were dry, they were cut into separate pages. Then the printer could arrange the pages in order and bind them.

Part of the printer's job was to edit and proofread the material they printed. Some customers even asked printers to write advertisements or articles for them.

Benjamin worked as a printer's apprentice for his older brother, James Franklin. Benjamin soon discovered that he enjoyed the printing business.

Benjamin also came up with a plan to improve his own writing skills. He studied essays published in a London newspaper. He made notes about how each paragraph was written. He tried to understand what made the writing so good. Then Benjamin tried to imitate what he had read.

Published Writer

In 1721, James Franklin started a newspaper, *The New-England Courant*. He printed local news and essays criticizing the government or church leaders for being too strict. These essays—written by James and his friends—were published under silly, made-up names.

Benjamin decided to try writing something for the paper. He disguised his handwriting and wrote:

> Sir,
> It may not be improper in the first Place to inform your Readers, that I intend once a Fortnight [two weeks] to present them, by the Help of this Paper, with a short Epistle [message], which I presume will add somewhat to their Entertainment.
> And since it is observed, that [most] . . . People, now a days, are unwilling either to commend or dispraise what they read, until they are in some measure informed who or what the Author of it is, whether he be *poor* or *rich, old* or *young,* a *Schollar* (sic) or a *Leather Apron Man* . . . it may not be amiss to begin with a short Account of my past Life and present Condition.[5]

After writing the history of his character's life, the young author signed the letter "Silence Dogood." He slipped the letter under the shop door and waited to see what would happen.

James printed the letter. Benjamin was thrilled when his brother and friends discussed how well it was written. He was especially pleased when they guessed at who might have written the letter. Only names of important citizens of "Learning and Ingenuity" were mentioned.[6]

Benjamin wrote thirteen more letters poking fun at topics such as religious hypocrites and town drunks. He even wrote one letter suggesting that women should have the same rights as men. After fourteen letters, Benjamin finally told James that he was the author. James was not pleased that his younger brother had fooled him.

I am . . . a mortal Enemy to arbitrary [changeable] Government and unlimited Power. I am naturally very jealous for the Rights and Liberties of my Country, and the least Appearance of an Incroachment [that someone was taking away] . . . those invaluable Privileges [rights] is apt to make my Blood boil exceedingly.[7]

At sixteen, Benjamin wrote this Silence Dogood letter calling for limited government power and the protection of citizens' rights. These ideas eventually became part of the United States Constitution, which he helped to write.

In the spring of 1722, an item printed in *The New-England Courant* angered the church and government leaders. James Franklin was thrown in jail. Benjamin ran the paper while his brother was in prison. This experience showed Benjamin how much he had learned during his five years as an apprentice. Now, Benjamin wanted to be released from his apprenticeship.

When James got out of jail, the two brothers argued frequently. Their father usually sided with

James, and Benjamin finally decided to run away. He sold some books to raise money and secretly planned his escape. Benjamin set sail for New York "near 300 Miles from home," he later said in his autobiography, ". . . a Boy of but 17, without the least Recommendation to or Knowledge of any Person in the Place, and with very little Money in my Pocket."[8]

That was not the end of his journey, however. When he could not find work as a printer in New York City, Benjamin traveled west to the colony of Pennsylvania and the city he would call home for the rest of his life—Philadelphia.

Philadelphia

WHEN HE LEFT New York, Franklin had little money left. He paid for two ferry rides across the Hudson and Raritan rivers, and then walked to Burlington, New Jersey. From there, he helped row a small boat down the Delaware River to Philadelphia. The boat landed at the Market Street wharf in October 1723. He later wrote, "I was dirty from my journey; my pockets were stuffed out with shirts and stockings, and I knew no soul nor where to look for lodging."[1]

Franklin bought three large rolls from a bakery with the little money he had. With his pockets already full, he tucked one roll under his right arm, one under his left, and ate the other as he walked along Market Street. Soon he began to realize how silly he must look. He was even more embarrassed when he noticed a girl about his own age watching him.[2]

Franklin quickly found a job working for Samuel Keimer, one of the two town printers. His next problem was finding a place to live. Keimer suggested that the John Read family might take in a boarder. Franklin did find a place to stay at the Read home. He also met Deborah Read—the fifteen-year-old girl he had noticed on his first morning in Philadelphia. Franklin looked more respectable by this time. His trunk had arrived and he was dressed in clean clothes.

Promising Future

During his first winter in Philadelphia, Franklin lived "very agreeably, forgetting Boston as much as I could."[3] He did not let anyone know where he was. His brother-in-law, Robert Holmes, eventually learned that Franklin was in Philadelphia and wrote to tell him how worried the family was. He asked Franklin to come home.

Franklin sent a reply saying that he did not wish to return to Boston. It was read by a guest of Franklin's brother-in-law, Sir William Keith. The young man's writing style impressed Keith, the governor of Pennsylvania. He decided to look Franklin up when he returned to Philadelphia.

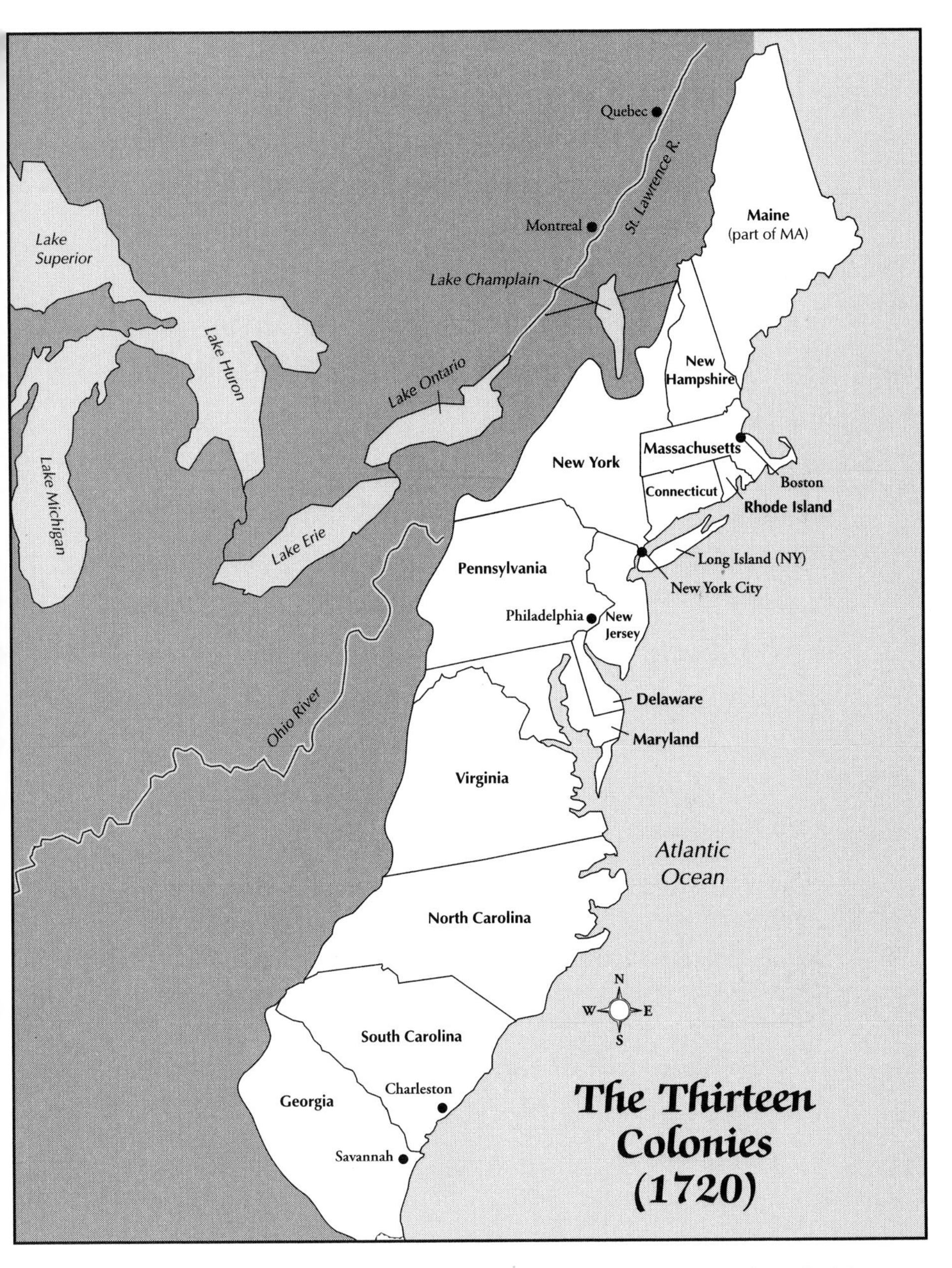

This map shows the thirteen American colonies and major colonial cities. After leaving the colony of Massachusetts, Benjamin Franklin arrived in Philadelphia, a busy seaport in the colony of Pennsylvania.

The governor thought little of the skills of the printers in the city at the time. He felt that Franklin showed a special talent and encouraged the young man to open his own shop. Franklin believed that he could run his own business. Unfortunately, he had no money to pay for a press and the other equipment needed to set up shop. Encouraged by Keith, he finally decided to ask his father for a loan.

In April 1724, after being gone for seven months without telling his family where he was, Franklin sailed back to Boston. Everyone except James was glad to see him.[4] They had feared that he was dead.

During the visit, Franklin asked Josiah to loan him money to open a print shop. His father refused. He understood the responsibilities of running a business. He felt that his eighteen-year-old son was too young. Franklin left for Philadelphia with his family's good wishes, but without the money.

Keith was disappointed that Josiah would not help his son, but he continued to encourage the young man. Finally, the governor agreed to provide the funds. Franklin booked passage on a ship to London. There, he could purchase printing equipment.

As he made plans for his business, Franklin also fell in love. His sweetheart was Deborah Read. The young couple discussed marriage. However, Sarah Read, Deborah's mother, asked them to wait until Franklin returned from England.

London

Franklin set sail on November 5, 1724. He expected to return to Philadelphia in about six months. Then he would open his own print shop and marry Deborah. Unfortunately, he discovered some problems after the ship had sailed. Governor Keith had not delivered letters to introduce Franklin to people in London as he had promised. Franklin had hoped to stay with Keith's friends during his stay. More importantly, there was no letter of credit. This paper would permit Franklin to charge the cost of the equipment and supplies he needed to Keith's personal accounts.

Franklin explained this problem to his cabin mate, Thomas Denham. Denham had known Keith for a long time. He explained that the governor was in debt and could not possibly provide a letter of credit.

When the ship reached London, Franklin had little money—definitely not enough for a ticket home. He had no friends in the city. It was clear that he needed to find a job. Luckily, there were many printers in London, and he found work quickly.

With no idea when he could return to Philadelphia, Franklin also gave up his plans to marry Deborah Read. He wrote to her only once ". . . to let her know I was not likely soon to return."[5]

During his time in London, Franklin read as much as he could. He also met several British authors and scientists. However, after two years, Franklin grew "tired of London . . . [He] remembered with pleasure the happy months . . . spent in Pennsylvania, and wished again to see it."[6] He began saving money and looking for a way to get home.

The Journey Home

In 1726, Thomas Denham, Franklin's cabin mate on the voyage to London, decided to open a store in Philadelphia. He offered the young man a job as a clerk and bookkeeper. This was his ticket home, and Franklin accepted the offer. On July 23, the twenty-year old and his employer set sail for America. During the voyage, Franklin kept a daily journal, entitled ". . . Occurrences [happenings] in My Voyage to Philadelphia."[7] He recorded information about fish, birds, wind, and any eclipses of the sun or moon that he saw.

When the ship docked in Philadelphia, Franklin immediately went to work learning his new trade. Denham taught him about the business like a father training his own son. There were even plans for Franklin to someday be Denham's partner. Unfortunately, during the winter of 1727, Denham died of an unknown illness, and Franklin was again looking for work.

In Business for Himself

Franklin went back to work for Keimer, the first printer he had worked for in Philadelphia. Keimer asked Franklin to run his print shop and train the other workers. After a few months, Keimer began to quarrel with Franklin, and the young man looked for another opportunity.

Franklin decided to open a print shop with Hugh Meredith, one of the workers he had trained. Meredith's father loaned them the money needed for equipment and supplies. Franklin brought his experience to the partnership.

In 1729, Franklin started a newspaper, *The Pennsylvania Gazette*. He wrote and published articles and amusing letters. He also advertised goods and services. Many people read his paper—even members of the Pennsylvania Assembly, the colonial governing body.

After a few months, Franklin began to have problems with his partner. Meredith drank too much. He began to spend less and less time at work. In July 1730, Franklin decided to buy his partner's

After sailing to England, Franklin found himself unable to pay for his passage home. As a result, he was forced to abandon plans to marry Deborah Read.

share of the shop.[8] At the age of twenty-four, Franklin finally owned his own business.

A Family Man

Now the owner of his own print shop, Franklin decided it was time to marry. He again asked Deborah Read to be his wife. Deborah had married John Rogers while Franklin was in London, but Rogers had turned out to be a poor choice. He soon deserted her and fled to the West Indies. There were rumors that Rogers had died, but Deborah had no proof. Divorce was not legal at the time in Pennsylvania.

Benjamin Franklin used this printing press in his Philadelphia print shop.

Because of Deborah's situation, the Franklins did not have a church wedding. Instead, on September 1, 1730, they began living together as husband and wife. This was known as a common-law marriage, a situation which occurred frequently during colonial times.

Franklin appreciated his wife and her ability to manage on a small budget. Over fifty years later, he wrote to a friend, "Frugality [thriftiness] is an enriching virtue, a virtue I never could acquire in myself, but I was once lucky enough to find it in a wife, who thereby became a fortune to me."[9]

Deborah agreed to raise William, Franklin's infant son. (William's birth mother is not known.) Deborah and Franklin's first child was born on October 20, 1732. They named him Francis Folger Franklin. They had one other child, Sarah, born eleven years later in 1743.

Poor Richard's Almanac

In 1732, Franklin and Deborah paid off all their debts. Now they owned the print shop free and clear. That same year, Franklin decided to write and print *Poor Richard's Almanac* (spelled "Almanack" back then).

The first issue was published in December. Like other almanacs of the time, it listed the tides and forecast the weather. It included a mixture of recipes, jokes, poems, proverbs, and unusual facts. But the witty voice of Franklin's imaginary author, Richard Saunders, made this almanac special. When the first copies sold out quickly, Franklin knew he had a successful project.

Every almanac offered words of wisdom on daily living. Franklin filled all the little spaces with proverbs or sayings. Some of his sayings included:

> A penny saved is a penny earned.
> An apple a day keeps the doctor away.
> Fish and visitors smell in three days.
> Nothing is certain but death and taxes.

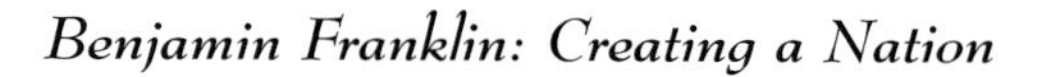

Almanacs

Almanacs are still printed today. They are based on the calendar. During Franklin's time, almanac writers included all kinds of information to interest different types of people.

Farmers relied on almanacs to forecast the last frost, after which it was probably safe to plant crops. Travelers studied the chart that showed the phases of the moon. With no modern streetlights, they depended on moonlight if they had to travel at night. Ship captains studied tide charts to learn the best times to set sail.

Dates of important religious holidays were also listed in the almanac. It "came into almost as many hands as the *best of books* [The Bible],"[10] according to Boston minister Cotton Mather.

Poor Richard, 1733.
AN
Almanack
For the Year of Chrift
1733,
Being the Firft after LEAP YEAR:

And makes fince the Creation — Years
By the Account of the Eastern *Greeks* — 7241
By the Latin Church, when ☉ ent. ♈ — 6932
By the Computation of *W. W.* — 5742
By the *Roman* Chronology — 5682
By the *Jewish* Rabbies — 5494

Wherein is contained
The Lunations, Eclipfes, Judgment of the Weather, Spring Tides, Planets Motions & mutual Afpects, Sun and Moon's Rifing and Setting, Length of Days, Time of High Water, Fairs, Courts, and obfervable Days.
Fitted to the Latitude of Forty Degrees, and a Meridian of Five Hours Weft from *London*, but may without fenfible Error, ferve all the adjacent Places, even from *Newfoundland* to *South-Carolina*.
By *RICHARD SAUNDERS*, Philom.
PHILADELPHIA:
Printed and fold by *B. FRANKLIN*, at the New Printing-Office near the Market.

Poor Richard's Almanac, *like other almanacs of the time, listed the tides, forecast the weather, and included various facts.*

Franklin, twenty-six years old, had been well known in the community of Philadelphia for some time. And as orders for *Poor Richard's Almanac* poured in from all over, the name of Benjamin Franklin was soon recognized throughout the thirteen English colonies.

Community Leader and Scientist

DURING HIS TWENTIES, Franklin worked hard to make his print shop successful. Then for the next several years, he found time to work on public projects. Members of a discussion group he had organized when he was only twenty helped him. This group of men, called the Junto, met to discuss religion, politics, and science. Members also believed that writing was an important skill. Every three months, each member wrote and read an essay to the group. Then others would suggest ways in which the author could improve his ideas and writing style. Franklin was one of the youngest of the group, but other members often followed his lead.

First Public Library

One of the first ideas the Junto worked on was a lending library. Franklin suggested that Junto members donate books they owned. The books would be kept in a room they rented for meetings. Franklin believed these books "would not only be ready to consult in our conferences, but become a common benefit, each of us being at liberty to borrow such as he wished to read at home."[1]

Members who could not donate books paid a small fee to use the library. The fee was used to buy new books. Anyone could visit the room and look at the books, but only members could borrow them. Within four months, the library had fifty members. A librarian was hired, and a new room

Benjamin Franklin and other members of the Junto donated books for a lending library.

was rented to house the collection. The library, Franklin's first public project, was very successful. Years later he wrote that it was "the mother of all the North American subscription libraries now so numerous."[2]

Volunteer Firefighters

While in London, Franklin saw how fire had destroyed huge sections of the city. He feared that parts of Philadelphia would someday burn to the ground, so he penned an anonymous letter to the editor. It was published in his newspaper. In the letter, he wrote that "an ounce of prevention is worth a pound of cure."[3] This meant that Philadelphians should be prepared for a fire before one actually occurred.

Franklin suggested that Philadelphians form fire-fighting groups. Members would train regularly. They would learn to handle a fire engine in emergencies. They would also practice using equipment such as axes and hooks. A volunteer fire officer would lead each group. It would be his job to direct members when they fought a blaze. Members of the company would provide their own equipment. These tools were to be used only for fighting fires. Members would meet monthly for inspection and practice.

In 1736, Franklin and some of his friends from the Junto and library organized the first volunteer fire group in Philadelphia. The Union Fire

Company had thirty members. Every member agreed "to keep always in good order and fit for use a certain number of leather buckets, with strong bags and baskets which were to be brought to every fire."[4] Members were fined if they showed up for meetings without these supplies.

Franklin's company used the fines to buy equipment. In 1743, it bought a hand pumper, a fire engine like those Franklin had seen in London. Other citizens started more fire-fighting groups. Soon one group or another protected most parts of the city. Franklin was proud to have helped to protect Philadelphia.[5]

Other Public Projects

Franklin suggested that the city use taxes to pay for garbage collectors and policemen. He wanted shopkeepers to hire a street sweeper for the market. The money to pay for this would be raised by subscriptions, or contributions from all the merchants.

Franklin always believed that education was important. In January 1751, he opened an academy, or school, for the colony's young people. He was the school's president for the first five years. The academy eventually became the University of Pennsylvania.

In 1743, the Union Fire Company bought a hand pumper, an early fire engine. It probably looked like this model.

Family Matters

The Franklins were living comfortably with their two sons. The oldest, William, was nicknamed Billy. The family called Francis, the younger child, Frankie.

Then in 1736, a smallpox epidemic swept through Philadelphia. At that time, there were vaccinations for the deadly disease, but the Franklin boys had not been inoculated. As a child, Franklin had always been healthy. He was not especially worried about the disease. However, in the fall of 1736, Frankie came down with smallpox and died. Franklin never completely forgave himself for his son's death.

Seven years after Frankie's death, in the summer of 1743, Franklin and Deborah had a daughter, Sarah. Franklin made sure that his daughter was inoculated for smallpox before she was three years old.

Franklin also helped found the Pennsylvania Hospital. This hospital has often been called America's "first medical center."[6]

Under Attack . . .

During the 1740s, England was at war with Spain and France. The American colonies came under attack. In November 1745, three hundred French Canadians and two hundred American Indians attacked American colonists in Saratoga, New York. Thirty settlers were killed. Many more were taken captive. Anything the attackers could not carry away was burned to the ground.

News of the raid reached Philadelphia. The Pennsylvania governor called up the militia. He ordered them to invade Canada and rescue the captives. Fifteen-year-old William Franklin volunteered to go.

Franklin was now forty years old. He had no desire to fight, but he did support the idea of colonial defense. In the fall of 1747, he wrote and published a pamphlet entitled "Plain Truth." The pamphlets quickly sold out and had to be reprinted.

In "Plain Truth," Franklin pointed out how the wealthy city of Philadelphia might be attacked. He was also afraid that the French and American Indians would raid Pennsylvania farms and settlements along the frontier.

The Colony of Pennsylvania

King Charles II owed William Penn 16,000 pounds. In return for this debt, Penn asked Charles II to repay the debt with land in North America. He wanted to start a colony. It would be a safe place for his Quaker friends to live and worship. This religious group's beliefs were unpopular at the time.

Penn's request was granted. The king signed the Charter of Pennsylvania on March 4, 1681. Although the king had given him the land, Penn decided not to build any settlements right away. Instead, he bought land from the American Indians who lived there.

Franklin encouraged citizens to form their own militia. More than ten thousand responded in Pennsylvania. They formed neighborhood companies and chose officers. Soon the companies were drilling (training with their weapons). Women's groups sewed flags and supported the troops.

The Pennsylvania Assembly would not fund the militia. To help, Franklin organized a lottery. Tickets sold raised money to buy cannons and to build a fort below the city.

This plan made Franklin popular throughout Philadelphia. He later recalled "the officers of the companies the made up the Philadelphia Regiment . . . chose me for their colonel; but . . . I declined that station."[7]

Penn appointed a governor and drew up a constitution for the colony. It included plans for a colonial assembly. Laws passed by the assembly had to be approved by the Penns. (Other colonies, called Royal Colonies, were ruled directly by Parliament and the king.)

By the 1750s, the Penn family often disagreed with the assembly. The Penns were only interested in Pennsylvania as a source of income. They received large sums of money from leases. Pennsylvanians realized that they were making the proprietors rich. They resented the fact that the Penns were not paying their fair share of the costs of operating the colony.

Franklin's plan did not please the proprietor, or owner, of the Pennsylvania colony. Thomas Penn believed that Franklin had shown colonists they could act independently of the colonial government.

Franklin had not set out to challenge the Penns. He simply wanted to see his city defended properly. The Pennsylvania colonists had learned that they could protect themselves without government help. This would be a valuable lesson during the next twenty-five years.

An Inventive Mind

By 1748, Franklin was a wealthy man. At the age of forty-two, he decided to retire from the printing business. He was interested in studying "natural philosophy," as science was called at that time. He was especially interested in electricity. He read all he could about the subject. He believed that lightning was a natural form of electricity. He flew a kite in a storm to test that idea. Using his test results, Franklin invented the lightning rod. This metal rod kept buildings struck by lightning from catching on fire.

During the 1740s, Franklin also invented a better way to heat homes. The Pennsylvania Fireplace—now called the Franklin stove—was freestanding and made of cast iron. This stove heated rooms more efficiently than fireplaces.

Franklin wrote a pamphlet advertising his new invention. The pamphlet read: "In these northern

Lightning Fame

In April 1749, Franklin wrote a theory about the relationship between lightning and electricity. He explained that drops of water in thunderclouds became electrically charged as they bounced around in the wind. Lightning, Franklin claimed, was the discharge of these particles. He also suggested that a person caught out in a thunderstorm should never stand under a lone tree. He explained that when lightning struck the tree, the electrical charge followed the trunk to the ground and to the person standing near the tree. "It has been fatal to many," Franklin said.[8]

Benjamin Franklin flew a kite during a storm to test his theory that lightning was a natural form of electricity.

The study of lightning and electricity made Franklin famous. The Royal Society of London, the most important scientific group of its day, recognized his work in 1750. By the 1770s, his studies had made him the most famous American in the world.

colonies the inhabitants keep fires to sit by generally seven months in the year. Wood . . . must now be fetched near 100 miles to some towns, and makes a very considerable article in the expense of families."[9] Franklin claimed that rooms heated more evenly with the new fireplace. He included a drawing of the fireplace and instructions as to how it should be installed.

George Thomas, the governor of Pennsylvania, liked Franklin's new design. He offered the inventor a patent. That meant that Franklin was the only one who could sell his stove in the colony.

Franklin turned down the offer. The fireplace became very popular. If Franklin had accepted the patent, he would have earned lots of money.

Franklin was fascinated by the world around him. His interest in science never died. However, he soon began to spend more of his time on political affairs. Problems were growing between the thirteen American colonies and their mother country, Great Britain.

The Franklin stove heated rooms more efficiently than fireplaces. Stoves based on this design are still used today.

Political Leader in Pennsylvania

BENJAMIN FRANKLIN HAD a rule about running for public office: "[N]ever ask, never refuse, nor ever resign."[1] In May 1751, however, he broke that rule. He applied for the office of Colonial Postmaster General.

In August 1753, Franklin and Virginian William Hunter were appointed to oversee postal delivery in the thirteen colonies. The two men shared a yearly salary of 600 pounds, which came from the postage they collected after they paid expenses. Franklin did not expect to make much of a profit as postmaster. Instead, he hoped to bring prestige to Philadelphia by serving as an officer of the Crown.[2]

Franklin's first act was to appoint his son, William, as the postmaster of Philadelphia. (Franklin had served in that position since 1837.) Then he began plans to improve the system. He worked out a simple way to keep accounts. He printed forms and instructions. These were sent to all local postmasters.

In Philadelphia, Franklin started the penny post. A postman delivered letters not picked up at the postal office on the day they arrived. Customers were charged an extra penny for this service. Franklin also created the dead letter office. If letters were not claimed after three months, they were sent to the Philadelphia office.

During 1754, Franklin visited all the post offices in the northern colonies. He met with the postmasters. He helped them put their accounts in order. Franklin studied the roads over which mail was carried. He selected the best routes for mail to arrive as quickly as possible. As the service became more dependable, many people began to send letters by post.

His job as postmaster made Franklin's name well known throughout the thirteen colonies, but it did even more. The improved postal system drew "the scattered colonies together," according to biographer Carl Van Doren.[3]

Elected to Office

In 1751, Franklin was elected to the Pennsylvania Assembly. He was reelected every year for the next ten years. He was so popular that he never had to campaign.

Franklin quickly became a leader in the Assembly, even though he rarely gave speeches. (He believed that he was not a good speaker.)[4] He preferred to work behind the scenes to change others' opinions. He liked to settle differences through compromise.

In 1753, Franklin was one of three commissioners chosen by the Pennsylvania governor to settle problems with the American Indians of western Pennsylvania and eastern Ohio. These tribes' lands

Benjamin Franklin's hard work as Colonial Postmaster General improved the postal system and communication methods between the colonies.

were being invaded from the east and the west. The English were crossing the Allegheny Mountains to build farms and villages. French trappers and traders were claiming territory in the Ohio Valley. As the tribes watched hunting grounds shrink, they began to attack the frontier settlements more often.

Franklin and the other commissioners set out for Carlisle, Pennsylvania, with wagons loaded with gifts. They also took guns, powder, lead, flints, knives, and rum. They met with chiefs from the Six Nations (sometimes called the Iroquois) and their allies—the Delaware, the Shawnee, and the Miami tribes. The commissioners learned that the tribes were ready to declare war on the French.

The Six Nations wanted English settlers to stay east of the Allegheny Mountains. In addition, they wanted only three trading posts in their territory, which would be run by honest traders. They demanded that powder and lead be sold at cheap prices. Franklin and his companions agreed in principle to three trading posts, but said they must discuss the terms with their government. The Carlisle Treaty was the beginning of Franklin's political career.

The Albany Congress

In 1754, the British government asked the colonies to meet in Albany, New York. This city was near the border of French Canada and the fur regions of

Franklin and the American Indians

Franklin appreciated the American Indians and believed that the colonies needed their friendship. He respected their way of life. He admired their gifts of speech-making and politeness during treaty ceremonies. He thought that American Indians deserved fair treatment.

Franklin realized that the American Indians were not the ones who broke treaties or made greedy bargains. As time passed, he believed that "almost every war between the Indians and whites had been occasioned by some injustice of the latter toward the former."[5]

the northwest. The purpose of this meeting was to work out a treaty with the American Indians. The delegates were also asked to plan a way to defend the colonies from the French.

Franklin was one of the four commissioners selected to represent Pennsylvania. His name was already known by the other delegates. He had earned recognition with his electricity experiments and work with the post office.

During the meetings in Albany, Franklin presented his Albany Plan of Union. The plan united the colonies for their own protection. It encouraged them to band together in a federation to build forts, "defend the frontiers and annoy the enemy."[6]

Franklin drew and published what is probably one of the first American political cartoons in his paper. It was a picture of a snake divided into eight pieces. Each piece was marked with the initials of a colony. "Join, or Die" represented Franklin's belief that the colonies needed to form a union for protection.

The plan called for one general government made up of representatives from all the colonies. It would organize defenses during war and make improvements for the common good during times of peace. Franklin even proposed that tax on liquor or tea be used to fund the government. Nothing in this plan called for independence. The colonists wanted British troops to protect them. They also expected Great Britain to pay for forts along the frontier. However, ideas found in Franklin's Albany Plan of Union would later become the foundation for the United States Constitution.

Though the main purpose of the Albany Congress was to negotiate a new treaty with the Six Nations, members also debated Franklin's plan. In the end, the Albany Congress did achieve its main goal. The tribes accepted thirty wagonloads of gifts and declared a renewed friendship with the colonists.

The delegates also decided to take Franklin's Albany Plan home to be voted on by each colonial assembly. Unfortunately, not one of the colonies voted in favor of the plan. They were all unwilling to give that much power to a general council.

At War Again

Later that year, the Seven Years' War broke out between France and England. The French who lived in Canada did not want to lose their valuable fur trade. They encouraged the American Indian tribes to attack British frontier settlements and forts.

In December, Great Britain sent General Edward Braddock and three thousand British regulars to the Virginia colony. His orders were to capture Fort Duquesne (located at the present day site of Pittsburgh) from the French.

The general met with Franklin. It was the postmaster's job to organize a way for the general to communicate with the colonial governors. During their talks, Braddock told Franklin that he expected to take the fort easily. The postmaster warned him to beware of an American Indian ambush. Braddock did not listen. Though Franklin disagreed with the general's plan, he did help with preparations. He hired 150 wagons and 259 packhorses to carry all the supplies the army would need.

Braddock and his army moved slowly west from Fort Cumberland (now Cumberland, Maryland). They had to cut a road through the forest. This would later be known as the National Road.

George Washington, a twenty-three-year-old major from Virginia, was chosen as Braddock's aide. Braddock had asked Washington to go along because he knew the territory well and could offer advice. Washington suggested that Braddock teach the British troops to fight frontier-style. He knew that the French and American Indians fired from behind the protective cover of trees and rocks. Unfortunately, Braddock did not listen to his aide. He believed that gentlemen did not fight that way.

The general insisted on marching on Fort Duquesne with drums beating and colors flying. His army of 1,460 men outnumbered the French and American Indians. He expected them to surrender without a fight.

Then on July 9, 1755, as the British crossed the river near Fort Duquesne, the French attacked.

More than half the British army was killed, and Braddock was wounded. Shot through the lungs, the general fell from his horse onto the battlefield. He died three days later. Washington escaped without an injury. After Braddock's defeat, the colonies feared even more for their safety.

General Franklin

In 1755, American Indians raided the backcountry less than 100 miles away from Philadelphia. Most settlements did not have troops stationed near enough to protect them. Entire families were scalped and killed.

The Pennsylvania Assembly was worried about the lives lost. On November 25, it passed a militia bill. It provided 60,000 pounds for defense against the American Indians. Franklin headed the committee to manage the funds.

More bad news soon reached the Assembly. A Shawnee war party had attacked the village of Gnadenhuetten (near present day Bethlehem, Pennsylvania). Most of the villagers had been killed. All the buildings were burned. It had happened the night before the militia bill passed. The village was only 75 miles northwest of Philadelphia. Soldiers were needed at once to protect other settlements in the area.

Franklin mustered his troops quickly. With son William as his aide, he set out with fifty men on December 18. For a month, he and his troops lived near the burned-out village in crude huts. The weather was freezing cold. Everyone—including Franklin—slept on the floor. Even at fifty, he believed this was part of a citizen's duty. He had three forts built in the area. The settlers were glad for the protection of Franklin's militia and addressed him as "General."

By the end of 1756, the colony was in more danger than ever. The French still held Fort Duquesne and had taken two other British forts along the frontier.

In 1755, Franklin and a militia built three forts near present-day Bethlehem, Pennsylvania, in order to protect settlers against American Indian attacks.

Problems with the Penn Family

As the French and Indian War continued, the Pennsylvania Assembly had to pay for its defense. It raised money by taxing property owners. Unfortunately, the largest property owner in the colony could not be taxed. The Penns, who lived in Great Britain, were the proprietors of Pennsylvania. Their family had received the original land grant from the king of England.

For many years, the Assembly had asked the family to help pay a fair share of the colonial government expenses. They wanted funds to cover the costs of making treaties with the American Indians. Franklin and other members of the Assembly had even tried to levy taxes on the Penn lands several times, but without success.

Finally, in 1757, the Pennsylvania Assembly decided to send an agent to England. They wanted their agent to try to get the tax rules changed. Franklin was asked to go because of his ability to negotiate.

Franklin took his twenty-seven-year-old son William when he sailed to England. Deborah refused to go. She was afraid of boats and sailing across the ocean. The ship departed on June 12, carrying the Franklin men across 3,000 miles of ocean infested with enemy ships. Twice their ship was chased by the French vessels, but outran them. Franklin did not let danger interfere with his curiosity. During the voyage he studied the ship's design, its sails, the way it was loaded, and its ability to sail swiftly over the waves.

On July 27, 1757, the ship docked in Falmouth, England. Franklin and his son set out for London immediately. As soon as possible, he began his work as the Pennsylvania colonial agent. It was a job that would require all his skills.

Diplomat in London

FRANKLIN HAD BEEN SENT to London to meet with the Pennsylvania proprietors, Thomas and Richard Penn. He also planned to meet with Great Britain's Privy Council, whose members served as advisors to the king. It was his job as colonial agent to present petitions for the Assembly.

His first task was to lobby for the Assembly's right to tax the Penn lands. Funds raised by these taxes would be used to cover the colony's expenses. Franklin soon discovered that his job would not be easy.

Friends introduced Franklin to Lord Granville, president of the Privy Council. Granville was polite to the colonial agent, but lectured Franklin on Pennsylvania's mistaken ideas about their constitution. He informed Franklin that the "king's instructions to his governors . . . are so far as relates to you, the *Law of the Land*; for THE KING IS THE LEGISLATOR OF THE COLONIES."[1] Franklin was unpleasantly surprised by Granville's way of thinking. He wrote the council president's words in capital letters when he recorded the conversation.

Next, Franklin met with the Penn brothers and their lawyer. The meeting was held in the middle of August at Spring Garden, the home of Thomas Penn. When Franklin tried to discuss the issue of tax, the Penns refused to negotiate. (Thomas had disliked Franklin since he organized the Pennsylvania militia in 1747. He felt it had been an act of treason and viewed Franklin as a dangerous man.)[2]

Franklin met several times with the Penns and their lawyer. They asked him to write a petition outlining the Assembly's requests. Franklin drew up a paper titled "Heads of Complaint" and gave it to the brothers on August 20.

A few days later, Franklin wrote a letter to his wife. In it he explained that his job required "both time and patience."[3] He also told her that he feared he would not be able to return home for at least another twelve months.

In fact, Thomas and Richard Penn did not answer Franklin's petition for three months. Then, instead of speaking to Franklin, the Penns' lawyer sent their reply to England's attorney general. As Franklin had feared, almost a year passed before he heard the final word on Pennsylvania's petition.

The Waiting Game

Meanwhile, Franklin settled into his new quarters. It was expensive to live in London, but the American agent felt he had to put his best foot forward. He hired a coach or horse-drawn carriage. He gave elegant dinner parties for friends. Franklin continued his electrical experiments in his bedroom. Sometimes he even dropped in at a nearby printing house to talk shop with the pressmen.

Pennsylvania proprietor Thomas Penn viewed Benjamin Franklin (pictured) as a dangerous man.

Though his family was in Philadelphia, Franklin did not forget them. He explored London shops and sent home two cases of gifts. He picked out a crimson satin cloak for Deborah. He also sent her English china, silver salt ladles, and a gadget to core apples. For daughter Sarah, Franklin purchased a black silk cloak, a muff (a fur tube to keep

ladies' hands warm), and linen fabric for a new dress.

During this time, William studied law. In 1760, he fathered an illegitimate son. William named the boy William Temple. The child would eventually live with Benjamin Franklin in his Philadelphia home.

The Penns' Compromise

Finally on August 28, 1759, the Penns offered a compromise. A small portion of their land could be taxed—lands that had been surveyed. Areas that had not been surveyed were not taxed. The king and Privy Council approved this plan on September 3. Franklin and the Pennsylvania Assembly had finally won the right to tax the colony's largest landowner. However, the tax collected was still quite small when compared to the amount of land the Penns held.

This small victory made discussions with the proprietors even more difficult. The Penns and Franklin continued to disagree over the rights of colonial citizens. Thomas Penn stated that the colony had no liberties except those specifically granted by the charter. In Franklin's opinion, this denied British citizens living in America their basic rights.

Through all this, Franklin had expected the House of Commons to support the colonist's rights. He believed that members sympathized with British citizens living in America. However,

Franklin was wrong. Most members knew very little about what was happening across the Atlantic Ocean. In fact, many believed that an army should be stationed in America to handle any uprisings. They also thought that colonial legislative powers should be limited.

By 1760, Franklin's tasks as Pennsylvania's agent were done, but he stayed in London for two more years. In letters home, Franklin described the theaters, symphonies, and art galleries. During the summer and fall of 1761, Franklin and his son spent two months in Belgium and Holland. They were back in London in October to see George III crowned king of England. By the time he returned to Philadelphia, Franklin was regarded as a spokesperson for the American point of view.

Return to Pennsylvania

By January 1762, Franklin decided to return to Philadelphia. England was still at war with France. Sailing across the Atlantic would be dangerous. He waited several months until a convoy—a fleet of ships—sailed for America.

Before he left London, Franklin learned that William was to be the next royal governor of New Jersey. William also planned to marry Elizabeth Downes in September. Franklin did not stay for the wedding.

In February 1763, William and his new bride arrived in Philadelphia. The young couple stayed a few days with the family. Then Franklin and William traveled across the frozen Delaware River to New Jersey. Franklin watched as his son was sworn in as the colony's new governor.

For the next year, Franklin's job as postmaster took much of his time. By 1760, the English had beaten the French in America. Britain controlled Canada. Franklin's first task was to set up postal service between New York and the Canadian cities of Montreal and Quebec. Franklin also traveled from southern Virginia to eastern New England inspecting local post offices.

Franklin and the American Indians

The war between England and France ended in February 1763. The Treaty of Paris restored peace between the two countries. However, the colonists and the American Indians continued to fight.

The British now controlled forts along the frontier. American Indians feared that more settlers would follow the soldiers west. During May and June 1763, bands of American Indians attacked and captured every fort west of Niagara (on the eastern end of Lake Erie). American Indian war parties roamed the Pennsylvania frontier and massacred settlers.

One hundred men, who called themselves the Paxton Boys, took revenge on innocent American Indians. They murdered twenty American Indian men, women, and children. The families were living peacefully under government protection.

Outraged, Franklin published a pamphlet in which he asked: "If an Indian injured me, does it follow that I may revenge that injury on all Indians? The Only Crime of these poor Wretches seems to have been, that they had a reddish brown Skin, and black Hair; and some People of that Sort. . . had murdered some of our Relations. . . ."[4] Many Philadelphians disagreed with Franklin's support of the American Indian.

The Paxton Boys soon decided to march on Philadelphia. They wanted to kill American Indians living peacefully in the area. Franklin was asked to negotiate with the mob. He talked them into turning around and going home.

London Again

October 1, 1764 was election day for members of the Pennsylvania Assembly. Franklin hoped to be reelected. Instead, he lost by less than twenty votes. It was Franklin's only defeat during his political career. He believed that his pamphlet about the massacre of American Indians had turned voters against him.

Even so, Franklin was quickly reelected as Pennsylvania's colonial agent. The Assembly now had a new petition to present to the king. They wanted to be governed by Great Britain, not by the Penn family. Franklin accepted the post. He

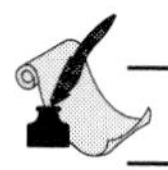

asked Deborah to go with him. She refused because of her fear of the sea. On November 9, 1764, the fifty-six-year-old civil servant sailed for England again.

The Stamp Act

As Franklin set sail, Great Britain's Parliament was trying to find ways to pay for the colonies' defense. They decided to tax British citizens in America. The Stamp Act made it necessary to buy a British stamp for every piece of printed paper used.

Franklin immediately spoke out against the Stamp Act, but it passed easily in the House of Commons. Then the House of Lords and King George III approved it. Colonists believed that Parliament had no right to levy taxes. After all, the colonies had no representation in Parliament.

The Stamp Act became law in March 1765. Citizens from New Hampshire to South Carolina demonstrated and rioted against the tax. Men hired to sell the stamps in America were threatened. Many quit, fearing for their lives.

Colonists decided to boycott British goods. Trade between Britain and America was cut in half. This hurt British manufacturers, merchants, and shippers. They also spoke out against the Stamp Act.[5]

Though Franklin had expected his countrymen to resist the Stamp Act, he was surprised and disturbed by the violence. Franklin nicknamed the act "the mother of mischief."[6] He worked hard to get it repealed. He wrote anonymous letters to the newspapers and encouraged others to do the same.

Franklin also testified before the House of Commons. He explained that Americans were willing to pay for their defense. They simply wanted their own assemblies to decide how the money should be raised. No one in London really understood this American way of thinking. However, the British respected Franklin's logical arguments. His statements, the colonists' demonstration, and petitions of English merchants convinced the British to repeal the Stamp Act in 1766.

The colonies celebrated this victory. Most Americans were so happy that they ignored the Declaratory Act, passed at the same time. This act stated that Parliament had the right to pass laws that the British colonies had to obey "in all cases whatsoever."[7] Franklin knew that the British government still believed they had the right to tax the colonies. It was only a matter of time before there would be another issue to argue.

Colonial Agent

Though Franklin had won a great victory, the Stamp Act created problems for him. His enemies in Philadelphia claimed that he had written the act himself and encouraged its passage. They accused him of accepting money for recommending stamp officers. Others thought Franklin had been promised a high post by the British government. These rumors led to talk of setting fire to the Franklin home. William urged his mother and sister to come stay with him in Burlington, New Jersey. Deborah sent Sarah, but refused to move herself.

The demonstrations in the colonies against the Stamp Act also made Franklin's work more difficult in London. Great Britain was losing patience with the colonies, and Franklin felt he had done all he could. He wanted to go home. However, the colonies of New Jersey, Massachusetts, Georgia, and Pennsylvania asked him to stay. The colonists were

His Daughter's Wedding

While Franklin was in London, his twenty-four-year-old daughter, Sarah, met Richard Bache, a New York merchant. Bache won Sarah's heart. Deborah Franklin gave her consent to their marriage.

The couple married in October 1767, while Sarah's father was still in London. Franklin feared that Bache was a fortune hunter, but he was too far away to stop the wedding.

Franklin's daughter, Sarah

already upset over another act. In 1765, Great Britain had passed the Quartering Act. They now expected the colonists to take soldiers in their homes and pay the expenses of an army in America.

Franklin also had another task to do for the Massachusetts Assembly. He needed to present a petition asking that Governor Hutchinson be removed from his post. So, while Deborah waited at home, Franklin stayed in London.

Turning Point

Franklin still believed that he could help the colonies and Great Britain find a friendly solution to their problems, but he made little progress. In 1773, he delivered Massachusetts' petition to the Privy Council. Then he had to wait and see if they would recall the Massachusetts governor.

The meeting with the Privy Council on January 29, 1774, was a turning point for Franklin. He knew that the Privy Council was upset. They were angry with him for sending Governor Hutchinson's letters to the colonies. He had expected some unpleasantness. But he certainly did not expect to be treated with a complete lack of respect.

Alexander Wedderburn, the council's lawyer, accused Franklin of stealing private letters and using them for his own purpose. He believed that Franklin wanted to be named the next governor of Massachusetts.

The colonial agent did not attempt to defend himself. He simply walked away. Franklin had entered the room a British citizen. He left as an American who knew there could be no compromise between Great Britain and the colonies. He realized that Parliament did not view the colonists as British citizens who deserved equal rights. Instead, Parliament saw them as subjects who should obey without question. From that point on, Franklin understood that America's only choice was independence.

Independence and War

BY FEBRUARY 1775, FRANKLIN decided that he had been away long enough. He made plans to sail home. Sad news arrived as he packed. Deborah, his wife of more than forty-four years, had died of a stroke in December.

Though Deborah was gone, Franklin looked forward to seeing his daughter Sarah and her family. After being away for almost ten years, he wanted to get to know his grandchildren. He headed home with hopes of enjoying a quiet life.

Time with his family was not in Franklin's immediate future. While his ship sailed across the Atlantic, British soldiers and the Massachusetts militia exchanged gunfire at Lexington and

Concord, Massachusetts. The thirteen American colonies reacted quickly. By the time Franklin arrived in Philadelphia on May 5, 1775, the Second Continental Congress had been called. Franklin was elected as one of the delegates from Pennsylvania. His new job began on May 10 in Philadelphia.

Delegates from each of the colonies attended the Congress. At sixty-nine, Franklin was one of the oldest members of the Second Continental Congress. George Washington was forty-three years old. Others who attended the meeting—Patrick Henry, Thomas Jefferson, John Adams, and John Hancock—were in their thirties.

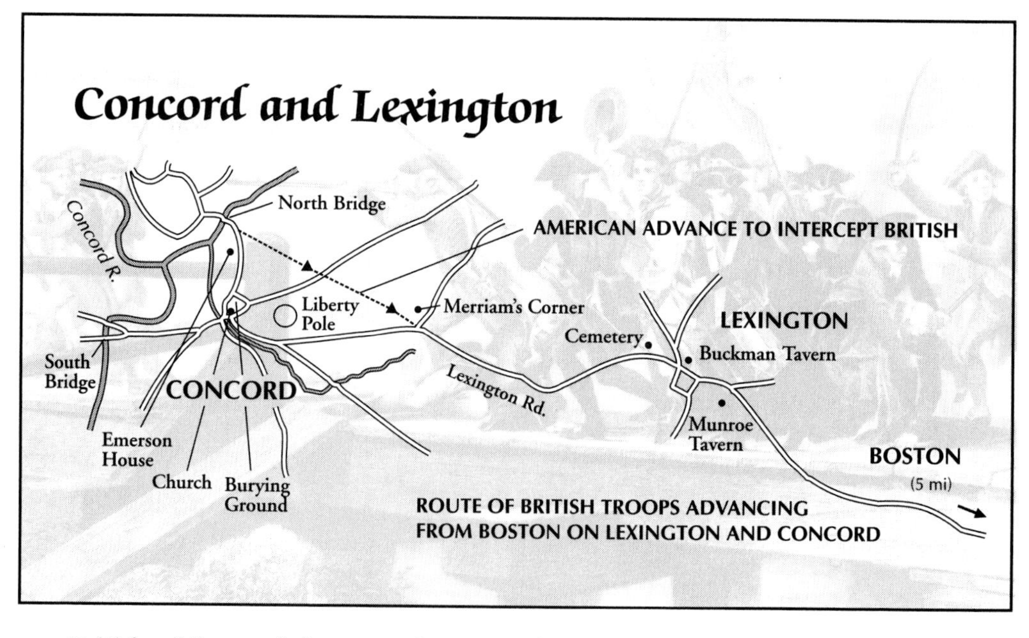

British soldiers and the Massachusetts militia exchanged gunfire in the towns of Lexington and Concord in April 1775.

The Shot Heard Round the World

On the night of April 18, 1775, seven hundred British soldiers marched toward Lexington and Concord. They knew the Massachusetts militia had guns and ammunition stored there. They hoped to surprise the colonial troops and seize the weapons.

However, Paul Revere was waiting to spread the alarm. He spotted two lanterns in the tower of the Old North Church. That signal told him that British troops were crossing the river by boat. Revere quickly rowed across the Charles River, mounted a horse, and rode to Lexington. He warned Samuel Adams and John Hancock that the British were coming.

When the British reached Lexington at sunup, about seventy minutemen were waiting. These volunteers had promised to be ready to fight at a minute's notice. No one knows which side fired the first shot, but it is often remembered as "the shot heard round the world." (The phrase comes from a poem written about the battle.) The shot sent a message to England that American colonists were determined to win their freedom.

Greatly outnumbered, the Lexington militia could not stop the Redcoats (the name the British soldiers came to be known by). The British marched on toward Concord. However, the colonists there had a surprise for the Redcoats. More than three hundred minutemen were waiting. They were armed and ready to fight. The Battles of Lexington and Concord were the first battles of the American Revolution.

Most members of the Congress did not want independence from Great Britain. One of their first actions was to draft one more petition to the king. They hoped that he would finally listen to their concerns. Franklin was certain that the appeal would do no good.[1] He believed that independence was the only answer for the American colonies.[2] He was ready to work hard to see that it happened.

On June 15, 1775, George Washington was named Commander in Chief of the country's armed forces, the Continental Army. Two days later, the army tried to drive the British out of Boston. They wanted to end the blockade of the harbor. The Redcoats won this skirmish, called the Battle of Bunker Hill. However, the British reported more than one thousand dead, wounded, or missing soldiers. Four hundred Americans died or were wounded.

Franklin had not wanted war, but said, "as Britain has begun to use force, it seems absolutely necessary that we should be prepared to repel force by force, which I think, united, we are well able to do."[3] He had no doubts that Americans would fight well.

Much Work to Be Done . . .

The Second Continental Congress gave Franklin many tasks. He was most interested in working on a new government for the colonies. Franklin went back to the plan he had written for the Albany Congress in 1754.

In July 1775, he proposed that the colonies unite for "common defense against their enemies" and "the security of their liberties and properties, the safety of their persons and families, and their mutual and general welfare."[4]

In his paper, *Articles of Confederation and Perpetual Union*, he outlined the duties for Congress, a new governing body. It could declare war, negotiate peace, and settle disputes among the colonies. Congress could also create new colonies, arrange treaties with American Indian tribes, set up a post office, and produce a currency or money system.

The number of delegates in Congress would be based on the male population of each colony. In this new draft, an "executive council" replaced the office of president-general. The Articles of Confederation defined the new government and was eventually adopted by the thirteen United States. It was based on Franklin's plan.

In 1775, Franklin was reappointed Colonial Postmaster General. He designed a paper currency. He also helped John Adams and Thomas Jefferson create the Great Seal used on all official documents.

In the spring of 1776, Franklin went north with three other delegates. They wanted to persuade French-Canadians, who were also British colonists, to join the confederation. It took twenty-seven days to travel from New York to Montreal. The seventy-year old delegate was worn out, and his legs were swollen when he reached the Canada.

Franklin soon realized that few French-Canadians were willing to join the American cause. They were content to be ruled by Great Britain. Canadians were also upset that Americans had already tried to free them.

Earlier that year, Congress had decided to drive the British out of Quebec and the area around the St. Lawrence River. They assumed that the French-Canadians would gladly join the thirteen colonies in rebellion. The Battle of Quebec was fought on New Year's Eve. Most American troops were killed or taken prisoner. Now, French-Canadians wanted nothing to do with the war against Britain. Franklin and his committee returned to Philadelphia without having gained their support.

The Great Seal of the United States was designed with Benjamin Franklin's help.

Franklin helped organize the Continental Army. He traveled to General Washington's headquarters at Cambridge, Massachusetts, and studied the army's needs. In November, Franklin became a member of the Committee of Correspondence.

Tories

Even after war broke out, many colonial citizens still thought of themselves as loyal British subjects. Those fighting for independence called these loyalists "Tories."

Colonial families were often divided over the issue of independence. It separated brother from brother, father from son. Franklin's son William was still the New Jersey royal governor. He did not agree with his father's political views. William refused to resign from his position. He also spied for the British, passing along information he learned from his father.

In January 1776, William Franklin was arrested for his Tory activities. He was tried and convicted as an "enemy to the country, and a person that may prove dangerous."[5]

Franklin sent money to his daughter-in-law, Elizabeth, when William was jailed. However, he did nothing to help his son. Franklin also left William nothing in his will.

This group had a big job to do. It was in charge of getting the weapons needed to fight a war against Great Britain.

Common Sense

Franklin had met Thomas Paine while serving as the colonial agent in London. He was impressed by the young Englishman and encouraged him to go to America. He even wrote letters of recommendation for Paine.

By 1776, Paine lived in Philadelphia. He was co-editor of the *Pennsylvania Magazine*. Franklin suggested that Paine write "a history of the present transactions."[6] Paine took his suggestion. In January 1776, Paine published *Common Sense*—his ideas on American independence. Paine sent Franklin the first copy of the printed pamphlet.

More than 100,000 copies of his pamphlet were sold that spring. In *Common Sense*, Paine stated: "The authority of Great Britain over this continent, is a form of government which sooner or later must have an end." In his pamphlet, Paine wrote: "In the following pages, I offer nothing more than simple fact, plain arguments, and common sense. . . ."[7]

According to Franklin, Paine's call for independence made a great impact on the members of the Continental Congress.[8] Washington was convinced after reading the pamphlet, but many others were not as sure.[9]

In May, Congress told the colonies to set up governments elected by the people. North Carolina, Massachusetts, and Virginia instructed their delegates to vote for separation from Britain.

On June 7, Richard Henry Lee presented a motion. He declared, "these United Colonies are, and of right ought to be, free and independent States."[10] John Adams seconded the motion. However, several colonies still opposed independence. The final vote was postponed for three weeks.

Meanwhile, Congress wanted a committee to write a declaration of independence, in case it was needed. John Adams, Thomas Jefferson, Roger Sherman of Connecticut, Robert Livingston of New York, and Franklin were asked to work on the draft.

The Declaration of Independence

Thomas Jefferson was chosen to write the declaration. Franklin gladly let someone else do most of the work. The trip to Canada had exhausted him. He suffered from severely swollen feet, skin rashes, and boils.

Franklin did agree to edit Jefferson's document, but he made only a few changes. One change was in a sentence stating that the king had agreed to acts "taking away our charters, and altering fundamentally [basically] the forms of our governments."[11] Franklin added the words: "abolishing our most valuable laws." This phrase pointed out that laws passed by the colonial assemblies were often vetoed by the king. In another section, Jefferson said that the colonial petitions had been "answered by repeated injury." Franklin suggested the phrase read: "answered only by repeated injury."[12] This made the statement stronger.

On July 1, the committee's draft of the Declaration of Independence was presented to Congress. The members discussed the draft sentence by sentence, making many additional changes. After nine hours of debate, it was clear that Pennsylvania, South Carolina, and New York would not vote for independence. Delaware delegates were evenly divided. Congress decided to postpone the final vote for one more day.

On July 2, the colonies were asked to vote for or against independence from Great Britain. The

Benjamin Franklin discussed the Declaration of Independence with other members of the committee: Thomas Jefferson, John Adams, Robert Livingston, and Roger Sherman.

delegates of South Carolina and Pennsylvania were still divided over the issue, but they did vote their support of the declaration. Another Delaware member (who supported independence) arrived in time to sway that colony's approval. New York was still waiting for instructions from home. Its delegates did not vote. However, when the votes were counted, there were more in favor of independence than against.

On July 4, 1776, the Declaration of Independence was formally adopted. Four days later, it was read aloud in front of the Philadelphia State House. The Liberty Bell was rung. Great Britain's royal coat of arms was pulled down from the building and burned.

The Declaration of Independence was copied, by hand, on parchment (animal skin prepared in way that it can be written on). Members of the Continental Congress officially signed the document on August 2. At the end of the ceremony, Franklin said, "Gentlemen, we must now all hang together, or we shall most assuredly hang separately."[13]

No Turning Back

The war did not go well for the Americans that summer. In August 1776, a British force under Admiral Richard Howe defeated Washington's army on Long Island. To avoid the capture of his entire army, Washington was forced to make a nighttime retreat across the East River to Manhattan.

IN CONGRESS, JULY 4, 1776.

A DECLARATION

BY THE REPRESENTATIVES OF THE

UNITED STATES OF AMERICA,

IN GENERAL CONGRESS ASSEMBLED.

HEN in the Course of human Events, it becomes necessary for one People to dissolve the Political Bands which have connected them with another, and to assume among the Powers of the Earth, the separate and equal Station to which the Laws of Nature and of Nature's God entitle them, a decent Respect to the Opinions of Mankind requires that they should declare the causes which impel them to the Separation.

We hold these Truths to be self-evident, that all Men are created equal, that they are endowed by their Creator with certain unalienable Rights, that among these are Life, Liberty, and the Pursuit of Happiness—That to secure these Rights, Governments are instituted among Men, deriving their just Powers from the Consent of the Governed, that whenever any Form of Government becomes destructive of these Ends, it is the Right of the People to alter or to abolish it, and to institute new Government, laying its Foundation on such Principles, and organizing its Powers in such Form, as to them shall seem most likely to effect their Safety and Happiness. Prudence, indeed, will dictate that Governments long established should not be changed for light and transient Causes; and accordingly all Experience hath shewn, that Mankind are more disposed to suffer, while Evils are sufferable, than to right themselves by abolishing the Forms to which they are accustomed. But when a long Train of Abuses and Usurpations, pursuing invariably the same Object, evinces a Design to reduce them under absolute Despotism, it is their Right, it is their Duty, to throw off such Government, and to provide new Guards for their future Security. Such has been the patient Sufferance of these Colonies; and such is now the Necessity which constrains them to alter their former Systems of Government. The History of the present King of Great-Britain is a History of repeated Injuries and Usurpations, all having in direct Object the Establishment of an absolute Tyranny over these States. To prove this, let Facts be submitted to a candid World.

He has refused his Assent to Laws, the most wholesome and necessary for the public Good.

He has forbidden his Governors to pass Laws of immediate and pressing Importance, unless suspended in their Operation till his Assent should be obtained; and when so suspended, he has utterly neglected to attend to them.

He has refused to pass other Laws for the Accommodation of large Districts of People, unless those People would relinquish the Right of Representation in the Legislature, a Right inestimable to them, and formidable to Tyrants only.

He has called together Legislative Bodies at Places unusual, uncomfortable, and distant from the Depository of their public Records, for the sole Purpose of fatiguing them into Compliance with his Measures.

He has dissolved Representative Houses repeatedly, for opposing with manly Firmness his Invasions on the Rights of the People.

He has refused for a long Time, after such Dissolutions, to cause others to be elected; whereby the Legislative Powers, incapable of Annihilation, have returned to the People at large for their exercise; the State remaining in the mean time exposed to all the Dangers of Invasion from without, and Convulsions within.

He has endeavoured to prevent the Population of these States; for that Purpose obstructing the Laws for Naturalization of Foreigners; refusing to pass others to encourage their Migrations hither, and raising the Conditions of new Appropriations of Lands.

He has obstructed the Administration of Justice, by refusing his Assent to Laws for establishing Judiciary Powers.

He has made Judges dependent on his Will alone, for the Tenure of their Offices, and the Amount and Payment of their Salaries.

He has erected a Multitude of new Offices, and sent hither Swarms of Officers to harrass our People, and eat out their Substance.

He has kept among us, in Times of Peace, Standing Armies, without the consent of our Legislatures.

He has affected to render the Military independent of and superior to the Civil Power.

He has combined with others to subject us to a Jurisdiction foreign to our Constitution, and unacknowledged by our Laws; giving his Assent to their Acts of pretended Legislation:

For quartering large Bodies of Armed Troops among us:

For protecting them, by a mock Trial, from Punishment for any Murders which they should commit on the Inhabitants of these States:

For cutting off our Trade with all Parts of the World:

For imposing Taxes on us without our Consent:

For depriving us, in many Cases, of the Benefits of Trial by Jury:

For transporting us beyond Seas to be tried for pretended Offences:

For abolishing the free System of English Laws in a neighbouring Province, establishing therein an arbitrary Government, and enlarging its Boundaries, so as to render it at once an Example and fit Instrument for introducing the same absolute Rule into these Colonies:

For taking away our Charters, abolishing our most valuable Laws, and altering fundamentally the Forms of our Governments:

For suspending our own Legislatures, and declaring themselves invested with Power to legislate for us in all Cases whatsoever.

He has abdicated Government here, by declaring us out of his Protection and waging War against us.

He has plundered our Seas, ravaged our Coasts, burnt our Towns, and destroyed the Lives of our People.

He is, at this Time, transporting large Armies of foreign Mercenaries to compleat the Works of Death, Desolation, and Tyranny, already begun with circumstances of Cruelty and Perfidy, scarcely paralleled in the most barbarous Ages, and totally unworthy the Head of a civilized Nation.

He has constrained our fellow Citizens taken Captive on the high Seas to bear Arms against their Country, to become the Executioners of their Friends and Brethren, or to fall themselves by their Hands.

He has excited domestic Insurrections amongst us, and has endeavoured to bring on the Inhabitants of our Frontiers, the merciless Indian Savages, whose known Rule of Warfare, is an undistinguished Destruction, of all Ages, Sexes and Conditions.

In every stage of these Oppressions we have Petitioned for Redress in the most humble Terms: Our repeated Petitions have been answered only by repeated Injury. A Prince, whose Character is thus marked by every act which may define a Tyrant, is unfit to be the Ruler of a free People.

Nor have we been wanting in Attentions to our British Brethren. We have warned them from Time to Time of Attempts by their Legislature to extend an unwarrantable Jurisdiction over us. We have reminded them of the Circumstances of our Emigration and Settlement here. We have appealed to their native Justice and Magnanimity, and we have conjured them by the Ties of our common Kindred to disavow these Usurpations, which, would inevitably interrupt our Connections and Correspondence. They too have been deaf to the Voice of Justice and of Consanguinity. We must, therefore, acquiesce in the Necessity, which denounces our Separation, and hold them, as we hold the rest of Mankind, Enemies in War, in Peace, Friends.

We, therefore, the Representatives of the UNITED STATES OF AMERICA, in GENERAL CONGRESS, Assembled, appealing to the Supreme Judge of the World for the Rectitude of our Intentions, do, in the Name, and by Authority of the good People of these Colonies, solemnly Publish and Declare, That these United Colonies are, and of Right ought to be, FREE AND INDEPENDENT STATES; that they are absolved from all Allegiance to the British Crown, and that all political Connection between them and the State of Great-Britain, is and ought to be totally dissolved; and that as FREE AND INDEPENDENT STATES, they have full Power to levy War, conclude Peace, contract Alliances, establish Commerce, and to do all other Acts and Things which INDEPENDENT STATES may of right do. And for the support of this Declaration, with a firm Reliance on the Protection of divine Providence, we mutually pledge to each other our Lives, our Fortunes, and our sacred Honor.

Signed by ORDER *and in* BEHALF *of the* CONGRESS,

JOHN HANCOCK, PRESIDENT.

ATTEST.
CHARLES THOMSON, SECRETARY.

PHILADELPHIA: PRINTED BY JOHN DUNLAP.

On July 4, 1776, Congress had a Philadelphia printer make 200 broadsides—poster-sized copies—of the Declaration of Independence. The copies were rushed to men on horses, who galloped off and delivered the news throughout the thirteen colonies.

Benjamin Franklin and other members of the Continental Congress signed the Declaration of Independence on August 2, 1776.

Howe thought that this defeat might encourage the colonies to lay down their arms and end the fighting. He asked Congress to send a committee to listen to a peace offer. Franklin, John Adams, and Edward Rutledge were selected to meet with Howe on Staten Island.

Howe offered to go back to the way things had been between the colonies and Great Britain before 1765. The colonies could elect assemblies and work with royal governors. Parliament and the king would again be the final authority. The offer came too late. The colonies no longer considered themselves colonies of England. They thought of themselves as independent states. Howe later claimed, "The three gentlemen were very explicit [clear] in their opinions that the . . . colonies would not . . . [agree] to any peace . . . but as free and independent states."[14] This ended the conversation.

Franklin was soon assigned to an even bigger task. Congress asked him to go to Paris. Franklin and two other delegates were to negotiate a treaty of alliance with France. Without aid from France or another country, the colonies would have trouble winning the war for independence.

It was a lot to ask of a seventy-year-old man who was not in the best of health. Franklin again had to leave the comfort of home behind and sail across the Atlantic Ocean in winter. If the British Royal Navy stopped his ship, he would certainly be recognized and taken prisoner.

Adams and Jefferson turned the job down, but Franklin agreed to go. He told a friend, "I have only a few years to live, and I am resolved to devote them to the work that my fellow citizens deem proper for me; or speaking as old-clothes dealers do for a remnant of goods, 'You shall have me for what you please.'"[15]

Franklin set sail October 26, 1776. Two of his grandsons—William Temple Franklin and Benny Bache—went with him. William would be his grandfather's companion. Benny was to go to school somewhere safer than Philadelphia, the rebel capital.

Franklin in France

FRANKLIN'S SHIP LANDED in France on December 3, 1776. He traveled to Paris—the French capital—by stagecoach. Two other commissioners, Silas Deane and Arthur Lee, joined him there. The three men asked for a meeting with French foreign minister, the Comte de Vergennes.

Vergennes arranged a secret meeting with the commissioners on December 28. The French were in no hurry to recognize the United States as an independent country. Battles had been lost along the Canadian border. Washington's troops had been defeated on Long Island. European countries—including France—wondered if the Americans could hold out much longer.

During the meeting, Franklin explained why the United States had asked to meet with the minister. They wanted to negotiate a treaty with France and Spain. Franklin also asked the French for eight warships, thirty thousand muskets, and ammunition.

Vergennes refused to loan French ships. He knew that Great Britain would consider that an act of war. For the next several months, he was also unwilling to begin official treaty discussions.

However, Vergennes did secretly help the Americans. French seaports were open to American ships. This allowed the United States to sell goods and purchase needed military supplies from the French. Vergennes also helped Franklin arrange for loans from French businessmen and the governments of France and Spain.

Even with French financial help, money was a constant problem for the United States. Congress approved the purchase of war supplies and the building of warships. However, when the bills were due, the commissioners discovered they did not have enough funds to pay them.

In September, Franklin, Deane, and Lee asked France and Spain for more money. Vergennes promised another small loan. He also hinted that France would take care of construction costs for the warships. He was still in no hurry to sign a treaty. The latest war news was not good. The British had forced General Washington to retreat across New Jersey and the Delaware River.

For the rest of the year, Franklin remained patient. He met regularly with the French minister and pushed for a treaty. On December 4, 1777, Franklin received positive news from America. The Continental Army had won an important victory. British General John Burgoyne had been defeated at Saratoga, New York, in September. Burgoyne and his army of 7,000 were prisoners of war.

With news of this American victory, the French were finally ready to negotiate a treaty—and so were the British. The British wanted to stop an agreement between the United States and France.

A Telling Comment

Throughout his life, Franklin was known as a man of few words. He listened more often than he spoke. This made his comments something people often remembered.

Franklin made a memorable comment while he was playing a game of chess with the elderly duchess of Bourbon. She illegally placed her king piece on the board. Franklin decided to make an illegal move of his own and captured her king. The Duchess realized that was not permitted. She told Franklin that in France "we do not take kings." With a sly smile, he responded, "We do in America."[1]

Great Britain sent representatives to Paris. Franklin listened to what they had to say. However, when he realized they still refused to recognize United States independence, he rejected their offer.

Franklin's meeting with the British did have one positive outcome. The French were ready to negotiate—and quickly. In February 1778, a treaty was signed. The French pledged support for American independence. America agreed to support France in a war with Great Britain.

Franklin had completed the job he had been sent to do. France joined the war on the side of the United States. Now all Franklin needed to do was to keep the money flowing. Most historians believe that the war could not have been won without financial help from France.

The War in America

After the American victory at Saratoga, the war again turned in favor of the British. At the Battle of Germantown, near Philadelphia, British forces defeated Washington. They captured the capital city of Philadelphia. British General William Howe spent the winter there in warm, comfortable lodgings.

Washington and his army were forced to make camp at Valley Forge, Pennsylvania. Already tired and hungry after the retreat from Philadelphia, the army had to build huts 14 by 16 feet to provide shelter from the cold. Food supplies were short, and the men had to make do with small rations. Food was

After the Continental Army won an important victory at Saratoga, the French government pledged support for American independence. Here, a treaty of alliance between France and America is being signed.

not the only problem Washington faced. There were not enough clothes and shoes to outfit his army. The general reported, "no less than 2898 men now in camp are unfit for duty because they are bare foot and otherwise naked."[2] Blankets were also in short supply, and men had to huddle around campfires to keep warm at night. "If the army does not get help soon, in all likelihood it will disband," the general said.[3] Washington finally decided to send out foraging parties to gather food and clothing.

Franklin did send Washington some needed assistance that winter. The young Marquis de Lafayette arrived in America at Franklin's request. This Frenchman served as Washington's aide. Franklin also sent Baron von Steuben, an experienced officer, to America from Germany. In order for Congress to accept this foreigner among the Continental Army's ranks, Franklin claimed von Steuben's position in Germany was higher than it really was.

With von Steuben's help, Washington drilled his men. Discipline improved and so did the soldiers' spirits. The arrival of spring and warmer weather also brought news Washington had hoped for. France had signed a treaty giving its full support to the American cause.

The French Fleet

In April 1778, the British evacuated Philadelphia. They marched back to New York City and prepared

George Washington and his army endured severe hunger and cold during their stay at Valley Forge, Pennsylvania.

United States Ambassador to France

Congress returned to Philadelphia after the British evacuated the capital city. They immediately picked an ambassador to France. They chose Franklin, now seventy-three years of age. He had already proven he could work with their wartime ally. Franklin became the first United States Ambassador to France.

to defend themselves from attack by the French fleet. On July 11, a fleet of sixteen French warships set up a blockade outside the city's harbor. Washington and his army crossed the Hudson River upstream from New York City. They set up camp at White Plains to keep the British from escaping north to Canada.

After nearly six years of war, Congress was ready for peace. They told Franklin and other representatives abroad to look for opportunities to begin peace negotiations. Franklin believed that peace would come only after the Americans soundly defeated the British. On October 17, 1781, Washington defeated the Redcoats in an important battle.

Battle of Yorktown

In 1781, Washington planned to attack the British forces holding New York. He changed his mind after a report reached his headquarters. His French aide, the Marquis de Lafayette, had been watching British General Charles Cornwallis and his troops. The general was camped along the Chesapeake Bay at Yorktown, Virginia. The British fleet was in the bay.

Meanwhile, a French fleet, under the command of Admiral Francois Joseph Paul de Grasse, was heading to that area. Washington realized this was his chance to corner Cornwallis. He prepared to march south. He headed for Yorktown with an army of twenty-five hundred Continental soldiers and four thousand French troops.

On September 5, the French fleet attacked. They defeated the British navy in Chesapeake Bay, and then opened fire on Cornwallis and his troops. The British general was trapped between Washington's armed forces and the French navy.

For the next several weeks, the Americans and French constantly bombarded the British. By the middle of October, Cornwallis and his troops were nearly out of food and ammunition. The British general had had enough. He ordered a drummer to signal that he wanted to talk with the American and French forces, but the guns were making too much noise. The Americans could not hear the drummer's signal. Finally, Cornwallis raised a white flag, and the guns stopped.

On October 19, 1781, General Cornwallis and 8,000 soldiers—one-quarter of the British troops in America—surrendered. This defeat ended any hopes Great Britain had of victory. By February 1782, Parliament voted to end the war against the United States. They were ready to negotiate a peace treaty.

The Treaty of Paris

When the news reached Europe that Cornwallis had surrendered his army to Washington, Benjamin Franklin believed his work was nearly over. His health was poor, and he wrote to Congress, "I have passed my 75th year." He asked that they send "some person to supply my place."[4]

Congress again refused to let Franklin retire. Instead, they appointed him as one of the peace

On October 19, 1781, British soldiers led by General Charles Cornwallis surrendered to American forces at Yorktown. This depiction of the surrender was painted by artist John Trumbull.

The First American

Franklin has been described as the first American. In 1776, he was one of the first founding fathers to believe that independence was the colonies' only choice. He also earned that title because of all the important work he did to build a working government for the United States.

Franklin did even more to change the American image abroad. At that time, Europeans thought colonial settlers were rough, uneducated backwoodsmen. Franklin set an example that gained their respect.

Franklin had been born and raised in America. His plain dress and fur cap symbolized the frontier lifestyle, and those who met him admired the fact that he had educated himself. They enjoyed Franklin's writing style. They valued his curiosity about the natural world. Franklin's friends in Europe enjoyed

commissioners. He was not happy to be given another task, but he accepted the job with a sense of duty.

John Adams, John Jay, Thomas Jefferson, and Henry Laurens were also named to the commission. Laurens was a prisoner of war in the Tower of London. He could not serve, and Jefferson stayed in America. Congress sent the commissioners these instructions. Great Britain must accept the United States as an independent and free country. This issue was not negotiable. On other matters, the three men were to use their good judgment. The listening to his common-sense wisdom. He was also respected as a businessman who had started with little and built a successful career. Today, many people around the world consider America the land of opportunity because of examples like Franklin.

John Adams, who personally disliked Franklin, wrote this about the statesman: "In address [the way he presented himself] and good breeding, he was excelled by very few Americans."[5] Franklin was extremely popular in France. French historian Simon Schama says Franklin's popularity was "so widespread that it does not seem exaggerated to call it a mania." He was "mobbed wherever he went . . . [Franklin] was probably better known by sight than the King, and his likeness could be found on engraved glass, painted porcelain, printed cottons, snuff boxes and inkwells."[6]

committee was also told to keep the French government informed about the negotiations.

When talks began, Great Britain's representative, Richard Oswald, suggested that American independence still needed to be discussed. Franklin disagreed. He made it clear that the issue of independence had been settled since 1776, when members of the Continental Congress signed the Declaration of Independence.

Franklin presented Oswald with a list of other issues that had to be included in any treaty. All British troops had to be withdrawn from America.

Boundaries of the thirteen states and Canada needed to be agreed upon. American rights to fish and to hunt whales off the banks of Newfoundland had to be guaranteed.

In October, the three American commissioners began meeting with Oswald. By November 5, they settled on a draft of the peace agreement. It contained all the points Franklin considered necessary. The British acknowledged the unconditional independence of the United States. Boundaries were spelled out for the United States and Canada. There

A warm reception awaited Benjamin Franklin upon his return from France on September 14, 1785.

was also an agreement on American fishing and navigation rights on the Mississippi River.

When the Treaty of Paris was signed on January 20, 1783, the American commissioners had won a victory of their own.

Home at Last

On December 26, 1783, Franklin reminded Congress of its promise to recall him after the peace treaty was signed. Another year and a half passed, however, before he became "once more a freeman."[7]

Franklin left Paris on July 12, 1785. He crossed the English Channel and sailed home from Southampton, England. Guns were fired in tribute to the statesman when he arrived at the Philadelphia Market Street wharf. Church bells rang out. On September 14, Benjamin Franklin had finally returned home. Now he hoped to spend the rest of his days in peace.

The Constitutional Convention

BY 1786, NEW PROBLEMS faced the independent United States. The country's new form of government was not working. The Second Continental Congress had drafted a thirteen-article document based on Franklin's Albany Plan. It was known as the Articles of Confederation. The government had worked under these Articles since 1781, when the plan was approved by the last state.

The thirteen colonies had worked together while fighting the English. However, the Articles of Confederation did not create a united country. The colonists had been rebelling against the rule of a powerful king. They did not want a strong central authority. Instead, their plan provided an opportunity for the states to cooperate. They could work together to defend themselves and to trade with each other. They could also send representatives to other nations. In all other ways, states operated like small countries. Each had its own individual constitution.

This caused many problems. European countries did not want to sign trade agreements with the United States. They knew Congress had no power to enforce them. In addition, the United States was practically broke. Congress could not issue money. Each state printed its own paper currency. When they ran out of money to pay war debts, they printed more. Paper currency lost its value, making it almost worthless.

Franklin and other political leaders saw the limitation of the Articles of Confederation. So did merchants and farmers. Some tried to modify the agreement, but changes required every state's approval. That was an impossible task. Citizens rebelled before leaders of the United States finally took action.

Shays' Rebellion

Massachusetts had a huge war debt. Legislators levied more and more taxes to pay these bills. Small farmers were hit hard by these new taxes. They usually did not sell crops for cash. They traded for food, clothing, and other necessary goods. When the state asked them to pay more tax, Massachusetts farmers banded together in armed groups to protest.

Daniel Shays, a former captain in the Continental Army, led one group of twelve hundred men. His band marched to Springfield, Massachusetts. Their plan was to capture weapons stored in the Springfield arsenal. On January 25, 1786, Shays and his men tried to seize the guns, but the state militia was waiting for them. The soldiers opened fire. Four protestors were killed. The others fled. Shays' Rebellion was over, and the news quickly spread to other states.

This event drew attention to problems that plagued the country. Political leaders realized that something had to be done. Many believed that if the United States was to survive as a unified country, it needed a stronger central government.

Call for Change

In February 1786, Virginia Governor Patrick Henry called for a meeting. He invited all the other governors to send delegates to Annapolis, Maryland. The purpose of the meeting was to discuss interstate trade problems.

The meetings began on September 1. Only twelve men—representing the states of Delaware, New Jersey, New York, Pennsylvania, and Virginia—attended. These men had not come to discuss trade problems. They had another purpose in mind. They wanted to make a formal request for a Constitutional Convention. They sent their request to Congress. They asked that a meeting be held the following May in Philadelphia. The request was granted.

The Constitutional Convention

Benjamin Franklin was now eighty-one years old. He hoped to spend his remaining years writing, reading, and in the company of friends and family. Once again, his wish was not granted. The Constitutional Convention began in Philadelphia in May 1787. Franklin was its oldest delegate.

Franklin and George Washington were both nominated to lead the convention, but Franklin's health was poor. He felt that his job was to listen, not lead. He asked Washington to serve as president.

Franklin did have some ideas about how the new government should be organized. He preferred one legislative branch. He wanted a committee to perform the duties of the president. He also thought that no officer of the federal government should be paid a salary.

Debate and Compromise

That summer, delegates to the Constitutional Convention debated the issues. They quickly agreed that the national legislature should consist of two houses. It took much longer to decide how

Franklin's Health

Franklin had bladder stones that caused him a great deal of pain. No doubt, he feared that he could not attend sessions every day. He was so frail that he had to ride the few blocks to the meeting hall in a sultan's chair. The chair, brought from France, was a seat mounted between two poles. Four prisoners from the Philadelphia jail carried the chair on their shoulders. If they walked slowly, Franklin's stones did not hurt him so much.

many representatives each state should have. Several plans were presented to the delegates.

Edmund Randolph, the governor of Virginia, presented one plan. He wanted the number of representatives to be decided by each state population. Under the Virginia Plan, states with larger populations would have more representatives.

New Jersey, one of the smaller states, had a different suggestion. The New Jersey Plan gave all the states the same number of representatives. The debate over this issue was heated. It nearly ended the convention before its work was completed. Franklin suggested a compromise, saying that:

> When a broad table is to be made, and the edges of the planks do not fit, the artist takes a little from both, and makes a good joint. In like manner here, both sides must part with some of their demands in order that they may join in some accommodating purpose.[1]

Roger Sherman took Franklin's suggestion. He introduced the Connecticut Plan. In this plan, members were elected to the House of Representatives based on the population of a state. In the Senate—the other part of Congress—each state had two representatives. Senators were chosen by state legislatures. (Today, voters elect them.)

This plan is remembered today as the "Great Compromise." This compromise guaranteed the success of the convention, but delegates still had a lot of work to do.

During the summer of 1787, the Constitutional Convention met in Independence Hall in Philadelphia.

Next, the delegates discussed who would run the government. They wanted a strong leader, but did not want any one person to have too much power. Alexander Hamilton still believed in the British system. He wanted to elect one man, who would serve for life.

Franklin believed that giving one man complete authority was asking for trouble. He also told members that life lasted beyond one's prime. Franklin wanted a committee to share executive powers. The convention again compromised between the two plans. They decided to have one man serve as president for a four-year term.

James Madison also suggested that administration powers be divided. Three parts, or branches, of the federal government would share them. These three branches were the executive, legislative, and judicial branches.

The legislative branch was made up of the two parts of Congress. This branch had the power to make laws, collect taxes, and borrow money. It would regulate trade with foreign nations and among the states. It could also coin money, set up post offices, declare war, and maintain armed forces. All laws had to be passed by both the House of Representatives and the Senate.

The president headed the executive branch. It was his duty to see that the laws passed by Congress were carried out. He headed the armed forces, made treaties with other nations, appointed government officers and judges, and signed or vetoed laws.

The third part of the new government was the judicial branch. It was made up of the Supreme Court and other federal courts. Its responsibilities were not spelled out in the Constitution.

The final issue of debate during the convention was how much power individual states would retain. This was also a challenging issue. Many states did not want to give up power to the federal government. It was finally agreed that both state and federal governments could levy taxes, but states could not print money. All powers not granted to Congress, nor denied to the states, were powers the states controlled.

Our National Bird

Franklin objected to the bald eagle as the United States national bird. He said that the eagle "does not get its living honestly . . . He watches the labour of the Fishing-Hawk, and, when that diligent [hard-working] Bird has at length taken a Fish . . . the Bald Eagle pursues him, and takes it from him."

Instead Franklin suggested a bird that was "not only native to America, but . . . industrious, and courageous"—the wild turkey.[2]

Franklin suggested the American wild turkey as the national bird.

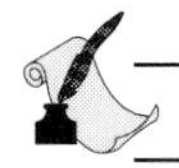

It was also agreed that the Constitution of the United States was "the supreme law of the land." If state laws differed, the Constitution prevailed.

The Constitution of the United States

After four months of debate and compromise, the delegates to the Constitutional Convention finally settled on a plan. Many Americans did not agree with everything in the final document. Most people had given something up. The founding fathers had compromised, however, to create a better government for the country.

In September, the completed copy of the Constitution was ready for the members' signatures. Franklin asked to speak to the convention. He reminded the delegates that although this document was not perfect, it was as perfect as they could make it:

> I confess, that there are several parts of this Constitution which I do not at present approve; but, Sir, I am not sure I shall never approve them; for, having lived long, I have experienced many instances of being obliged by better information or fuller consideration, to change opinions, even on important subjects which I once thought right but found to be otherwise. [. . .] Thus I consent, Sir, to this Constitution, because I expect no better, and because I am not sure that it is not the best.[3]

Franklin believed that no other convention could have done a better job.[4] He knew that agreement of all the delegates was impossible. Instead the members of each state delegation were polled. They decided to let the majority rule within each delegation. Using this plan, the thirteen states unanimously ratified (voted to approve) the Constitution of the United States.

On September 17, 1787, the delegates dipped quills into the same silver inkstand that was used to sign the Declaration of Independence. George Washington was the first to sign the Constitution. Thirty-eight other members of the Constitutional

We the People We the People We the People

We the people of the United States, in order to form a more perfect union, establish justice, insure domestic tranquility [peace], provide for the common defense, promote general welfare, and secure the blessings of liberty to ourselves and our posterity [future generations], do ordain [proclaim] and establish this Constitution for the United States of America.[5]

The founding fathers chose these words as the opening statement for the Constitution of the United States.

Convention followed his lead. Sixteen delegates decided not to sign.

James Madison remembered one final comment from Franklin about the sun painted on the back of the Washington's chair. Franklin said, "often in the course of the session . . . [I] looked at that behind the president, without being able to tell whether it was rising or setting. But now at length I have the happiness to know that it is a rising and not a setting sun."[6]

George Washington, who presided over the Constitutional Convention, was the first delegate to sign the United States Constitution.

Benjamin Franklin had done his part during the debate to create a workable government for the United States. Now, he could finally retire from politics.

His Final Days

Franklin lived the rest of his life with his daughter Sarah and her seven children. He was confined to his bedroom during his last year, but continued to write letters to old friends in America and Europe. Franklin followed the events of the

French Revolution and supported the cause of abolition.

Views on Slavery

In 1730, slavery had existed in all the English colonies. Franklin had not objected to running advertisements for runaway slaves in his newspaper, *The Pennsylvania Gazette*.

In his final years, however, Franklin served as the president of the Pennsylvania Society Promoting the Abolition of Slavery and wrote an essay making fun of Congressman Andrew Jackson's speech defending slavery. Before his death, Franklin decided that slavery was wrong and should be outlawed. He believed liberty was the right of all people living in America "without distinction of color."[7]

Loss of a Founding Father

As he grew weaker, Franklin was given opium, a drug. It eased the pain caused by a bladder stone. The medication often made him so sleepy he could not carry on a conversation. On April 17, 1790, only two years after the Constitutional Convention had completed its job, Benjamin Franklin slipped into a coma. He died at the age of eight-four.

Church bells tolled around the city. Members of the House of Representatives voted to wear black badges of mourning for a month. American flags across the country were lowered to half-mast.

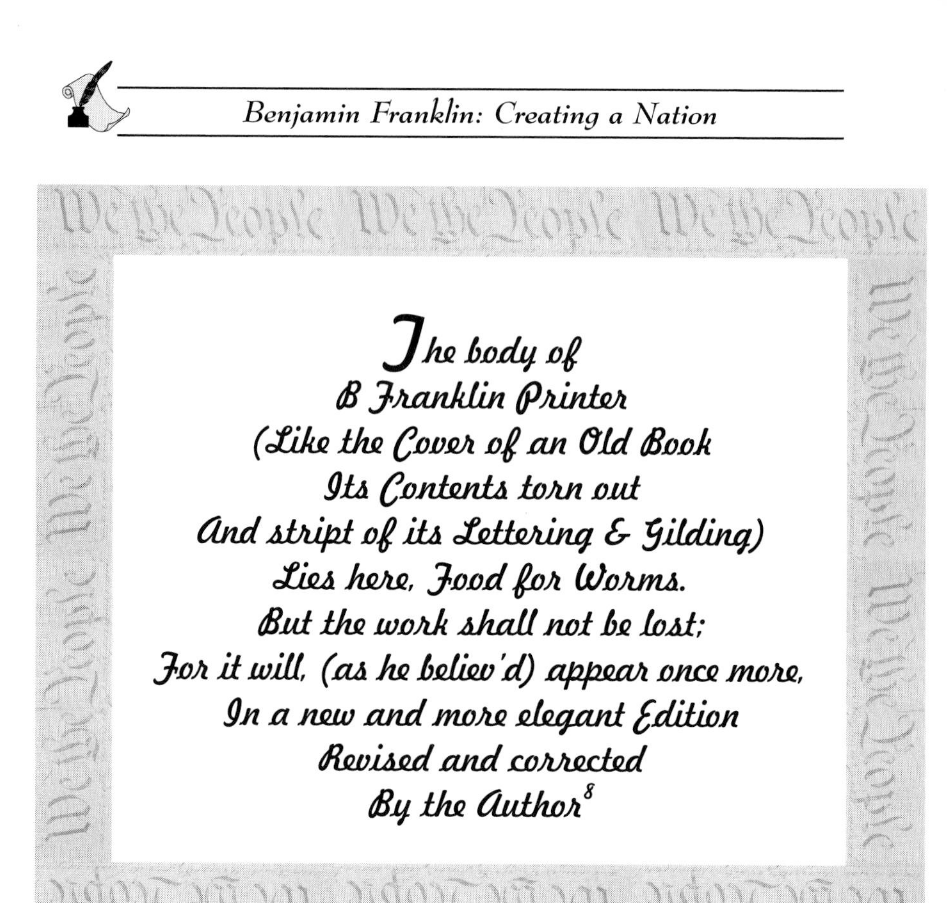

Although his grave is marked in a simpler manner, Franklin wrote this epitaph for himself sixty-two years before his death.

Twenty thousand people attended the funeral. His loss was mourned in France and other parts of Europe, as well.

The procession followed Franklin's casket to a grave at Christ Church in Philadelphia. He was buried beside his wife. At Franklin's request, a simple stone marked the site. It was engraved with these words: "Benjamin and Deborah Franklin, 1790." After dedicating his life to his community and country, Benjamin Franklin could finally rest peacefully.

One Founding Father

DURING HIS LIFETIME, Franklin's name was well-known in America and abroad. He was recognized both as a scientist and a statesman. Today, most Americans know his name. Franklin can be found more than one hundred times on the map of the United States. In fact, every state has a town named after him.

Many areas have Franklin streets and Franklin schools. Many businesses have adopted his name. These companies sell printing presses, stoves, paper, insurance, and even cars. Benjamin Franklin is remembered for all the things he accomplished during his life. Most importantly, he is honored for the work he did as one of our country's founding fathers.

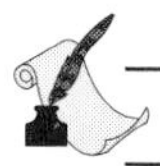

In Philadelphia

Franklin's first service began at the community level. A tour of Philadelphia today is like taking a walk in Franklin's footsteps. Visitors can walk through the room where Franklin attended meetings of the Second Continental Congress and Constitutional Convention. They can learn more about his experiments and modern science at the Franklin Institute. People can see Franklin's grave near Fifth and Arch streets.

Sightseers can also stop by Franklin's library. It is now the Philadelphia Free Library. The library has grown since it was founded in 1731. There are fifty-five locations throughout the city.

Tourists may also want to visit Franklin's school for young people. That school still operates today as the University of Pennsylvania. The University has earned honors for its excellence in education. On the bicentennial of Franklin's death, the University was 250 years old.

Another legacy Franklin helped found in 1751 is the Pennsylvania Hospital. It was twenty-five-years old when our country declared independence from Great Britain and is still operating today. Franklin's projects set an example for communities across our new and growing country. Today, most towns and cities have public libraries and hospitals that serve their citizens' needs.

Today, Franklin's school for young people has become the University of Pennsylvania (pictured).

Money to Grow on

Franklin's good works continued even after his death. In his will, Franklin set aside money for Philadelphia and Boston, the city where he was born.

Some of the money was to be spent on public works to improve both cities. However, most of it was to be used to help young men and women. Franklin remembered how loans had helped him start his printing business. He asked that these funds "be lent at 5-percent interest . . . to such young married artificers [craftsman] under the age of twenty-five years as have served an apprenticeship in the said town . . ."[1] After 100 years, the cities could use the money for other purposes.

After the first hundred years, Boston founded the Franklin Institute, a trade school, with Franklin's money. Philadelphia used the money to provide financial aid for science students. By the 200th anniversary of Franklin's death, the Boston fund had grown to $4.5 million. Philadelphia's fund was valued at $2 million. Today, grants and loans are still being made with Franklin's spirit in mind.

Building the Foundation

Long before the founding fathers began to dream of independence, Franklin worked on projects that helped unite the thirteen separate colonies. In his position as the Colonial Postmaster General, he improved mail service. This pulled the colonies closer together. The United States Postal Service grew from groundwork Franklin laid. Today, the system he started delivers mail from coast to coast.

Franklin also wrote one of the first plans to unite the colonies in 1754. His Albany Plan called for one general government made up of delegates from all the colonies. This government would organize defenses during war and make improvements for the common good during times of peace.

Push for Independence

During his lifetime, Franklin changed from a loyal British subject to an American patriot. He took a firm stand against Great Britain when it tried to deny colonists the same rights as other English citizens. He was one of the first founding fathers to believe that independence was the only answer. Because of this, Franklin earned the title "Father of the Revolution."[2]

At sixty-nine-years old, Franklin was the oldest member of the Second Continental Congress. His modified version of the Albany Plan was adopted as the first form of government for the thirteen independent states. Franklin designed the country's paper currency and helped create the Great Seal used on all official documents. Franklin also helped edit the Declaration of Independence. Then, he proudly signed the document on July 4, 1776.

Most historians agree that Franklin's work as a commissioner and later as a minister to France during the Revolutionary War was his most important contribution.[3] Without aid from another country, the United States could not have won the war. The Continental Army needed ammunition, arms, uniforms, and other supplies. They also needed loans to pay for it all. Franklin found the suppliers.

He obtained the loans. He also sent General Washington experienced military officers—Marquis de Lafayette and Baron von Steuben.

Franklin used all his negotiating skills to get France to recognize the United States as an independent nation. He was patient. If one approach failed, he tried something else. Franklin's persistence paid off. The French finally signed a treaty of alliance with the United States. That was a turning point in the Revolutionary War. With aid from the French army and navy, the United States finally had the weapons and power they needed to defeat British troops.

Oldest Member of the Constitutional Convention

In 1787, although his health was poor, Franklin accepted one last task as a founding father. He was a delegate to the Constitutional Convention held in Philadelphia in May. Franklin thought his role during this convention was to listen, not lead.

Whenever Franklin spoke the other delegates listened to his reasonable and practical ideas. The "Great Compromise" was reached after Franklin suggested "both sides must part with some of their demands in order that they may join in some accommodating purpose."[4]

Finally, after four months of debate and compromise, the delegates to the Constitutional Convention settled on a plan. Franklin again offered a comment

Franklin's image is displayed in the United States Capitol Building. It reminds visitors that he was one of the founding fathers.

before members voted. He reminded the delegates that this document was not perfect, but it was as perfect as they could make it. He believed that no other convention could have done a better job.

Benjamin Franklin worked tirelessly for the colony he lived in, and then for the newly independent United States. He always believed that reason and compromise could solve problems. He skillfully used those tools to build a solid foundation on a community, state, and national level. Franklin's spirit survives today in the lasting form of government that he and the other founding fathers created more than two hundred years ago.

Timeline

1700 — 1720 — 1730 — 1740 — 1750

1706
January 17: Born in Boston, Massachusetts.

1728
Opens a print shop in Philadelphia, Pennsylvania.

1729
Starts publishing *The Pennsylvania Gazette*.

1730
Sets up a common-law marriage with Deborah Read.

1732
Publishes first edition of *Poor Richard's Almanac*.

1736
Organizes the Union Fire Company.

1737
Becomes Colonial Postmaster General.

1747
Helps organize the Pennsylvania militia.

1751
Elected to the Pennsylvania Assembly.

1752
Performs electricity experiments.

1753
Helps negotiate treaty with Americans Indians.

1754
Elected delegate to Albany Congress.

1757
Travels to London as the colonial agent for the Pennsylvania Assembly.

1764
Goes to London as colonial agent for Pennsylvania, Massachusetts, New Jersey, and Georgia.

1765
Protests against the Stamp Act.

1773
The Boston Tea Party.

1775
April 18: Battle of Lexington and Concord.

May 5: Named to Second Continental Congress.

1776
January: Helps organize the Continental Army.

July 4: Helps draft the Declaration of Independence.

August 2: Signs the document.

1777
September 19: Continental Army wins victory at Saratoga, New York.

1778
February: Signs Treaty of Alliance with France.

1779
Chosen as first ambassador to France.

1781
October 18: Cornwallis surrenders to Washington at Yorktown, Virginia.

1782
Franklin, Adams, and Jay negotiate peace treaty with Great Britain.

1783
January 20 The Treaty of Paris is signed.

1787
May: Participates in the Constitutional Convention.

September 17: Signs the Constitution.

1790
April 17: Dies at the age of eighty-four.

1760 1770 1780 1790 1800

Chapter Notes

Chapter 1. Road to Revolution

1. Dr. W. Cleon Skousen and Dr. M. Richard Maxfield, *The Real Ben Franklin, part II: Timeless Treasures from Benjamin Franklin* (Salt Lake City, Utah: Freemen Institute, 1982), p. 184.

2. H. W. Brands, *The First American: The Life and Times of Benjamin Franklin* (New York: Doubleday, 2000), p. 6.

3. Esmond Wright, ed., *Benjamin Franklin, His Life as He Wrote It* (Cambridge: Harvard University Press, 1990), p. 202.

4. Brands, p. 454.

5. Ibid.

6. Wright, pp. 202–203.

7. Catherine Drinker Bowen, *The Most Dangerous Man in America: Scenes from the Life of Benjamin Franklin* (Boston: Little, Brown and Company, 1974), p. 235.

8. Ibid., p. 236.

9. Ibid., p. 237.

10. Skousen and Maxfield, p. 179.

11. Brands, p. 7.

12. Skousen and Maxfield, p. 180.

13. Brands, p. 7.

14. Bowen, p. 241.

15. Ibid.

Chapter 2. Boyhood Years

1. Catherine Drinker Bowen, *The Most Dangerous Man in America: Scenes from the Life of Benjamin Franklin* (Boston: Little, Brown and Company, 1974), p. 5.

2. H. W. Brands, *The First American: The Life and Times of Benjamin Franklin* (New York: Doubleday, 2000), p. 16.

3. Bowen, p. 8.

4. Benjamin Franklin, *The Autobiography of Benjamin Franklin and Selections From His Other Writings* (New York: Carlton House, n.d.), p. 15.

5. Ibid., p. 184.

6. Bowen, p. 21.

7. Franklin, p. 188.

8. Ibid., p. 24.

Chapter 3. Philadelphia

1. Benjamin Franklin, *The Autobiography of Benjamin Franklin and Selections From His Other Writings* (New York: Carlton House, n.d.), p. 27.

2. Ibid., p. 28.

3. Ibid., p. 31

4. Dr. W. Cleon Skousen and Dr. M. Richard Maxfield, *The Real Ben Franklin, part II: Timeless Treasures from Benjamin Franklin* (Salt Lake City, Utah: Freemen Institute, 1982), p. 22.

5. Ibid., pp. 46–47.

6. Ibid., p. 54.

7. Ibid., p. 222.

8. H. W. Brands, *The First American: The Life and Times of Benjamin Franklin* (New York: Doubleday, 2000), p. 105.

9. Skousen and Maxfield, p. 50.

10. *The History of Almanacs*, n.d., <http://www.gettysburg.edu/s469753/almanac/alman.html> (June 20, 2002).

Chapter 4. Community Leader and Scientist

1. Benjamin Franklin, *The Autobiography of Benjamin Franklin and Selections From His Other Writings* (New York: Carlton House, n.d.), p. 83.

2. Dr. W. Cleon Skousen and Dr. M. Richard Maxfield, *The Real Ben Franklin, part II: Timeless Treasures from Benjamin Franklin* (Salt Lake City, Utah: Freemen Institute, 1982), p. 58.

3. H. W. Brands, *The First American: The Life and Times of Benjamin Franklin* (New York: Doubleday, 2000), p. 135.

4. Franklin, p. 111.

5. Brands, p. 137.

6. Skousen and Maxfield, p. 85.

7. Ibid., p. 71.

8. Brands, p. 200.

9. Ibid., p. 166.

Chapter 5. Political Leader in Pennsylvania

1. Carl Van Doren, *Benjamin Franklin* (New York: The Viking Press, 1938), p. 210.

2. Ibid., p. 211.

3. Dr. W. Cleon Skousen and Dr. M. Richard Maxfield, *The Real Ben Franklin, part II: Timeless Treasures from Benjamin Franklin* (Salt Lake City, Utah: Freemen Institute, 1982), p. 95.

4. Van Doren, p. 205.

5. Catherine Drinker Bowen, *The Most Dangerous Man in America: Scenes from the Life of Benjamin Franklin* (Boston: Little, Brown and Company, 1974), p. 98.

6. Ibid., p. 131.

Chapter 6. Diplomat in London

1. Catherine Drinker Bowen, *The Most Dangerous Man in America: Scenes from the Life of Benjamin Franklin* (Boston: Little, Brown and Company, 1974), p. 166.

2. H. W. Brands, *The First American: The Life and Times of Benjamin Franklin* (New York: Doubleday, 2000), p. 187.

3. Bowen, p. 171.

4. Ibid., p. 183.

5. Carl Van Doren, *Benjamin Franklin* (New York: The Viking Press, 1938), p. 330.

6. Ibid., p. 334.

7. Ibid., p. 352.

Chapter 7. Independence and War

1. Carl Van Doren, *Benjamin Franklin* (New York: The Viking Press, 1938), p. 530.

2. H. W. Brands, *The First American: The Life and Times of Benjamin Franklin* (New York: Doubleday, 2000), p. 7.

3. Ibid., p. 500.

4. Ibid., p. 501.

5. Ibid., p. 525.

6. Van Doren, p. 548.

7. "Common Sense," *Thomas Paine (1737–1809)*, 1776, <http://www.bartleby.com/133/3.html> (July 8, 2003).

8. Brands, p. 510.

9. Esmond Wright, *Franklin of Philadelphia* (Boston: Harvard University Press, 1986), p. 244.

10. Ibid., p. 245.

11. Ibid., p. 246.

12. Ibid.

13. Ibid., p. 247.

14. Brands, p. 518.

15. Ibid., pp. 523–524.

Chapter 8. Franklin in France

1. H. W. Brands, *The First American: The Life and Times of Benjamin Franklin* (New York: Doubleday, 2000), p. 570.

2. Ibid., p. 572.

3. Independence Hall Association, "The Philadelphia Campaign 1777: What Happened at Valley Forge," *ushistory.org*™, ©1997–2003, <http://www.ushistory.org/march/phila/valley forge.htm> (August 15, 2002).

4. Brands, p. 591.

5. Bernard Cohen, *Science and the Founding Fathers: Science in the Political Thought of Jefferson, Franklin, Adams, and Madison* (New York: W. W. Norton & Company, 1995), p. 175.

6. Ibid., pp. 179–180.

7. Esmond Wright, *Franklin of Philadelphia* (Boston: Harvard University Press, 1986), p. 330.

Chapter 9. The Constitutional Convention

1. H. W. Brands, *The First American: The Life and Times of Benjamin Franklin* (New York: Doubleday, 2000), p. 682.

2. Ibid., p. 669.

3. Esmond Wright, *Franklin of Philadelphia* (Boston: Harvard University Press, 1986), p. 343.

4. Ibid., pp. 343–344.

5. The Constitution of the United States of America, Preamble.

6. Brands, p. 691.

7. Ibid., p. 708.

8. Wright, p. 348.

Chapter 10. One Founding Father

1. H. W. Brands, *The First American: The Life and Times of Benjamin Franklin* (New York: Doubleday, 2000), p. 713.

2. Edwin Wildman, *The Founders of America in the Days of the Revolution* (New York: Books for Libraries Press, 1924), p. 3.

3. Bernard Cohen, *Science and the Founding Fathers: Science in the Political Thought of Jefferson, Franklin, Adams, and Madison* (New York: W. W. Norton & Company, 1995), p. 171.

4. Brands, p. 682.

Glossary

alliance—An agreement signed by two countries for the benefit of both parties.

apprenticeship—An agreement to work for a specified length of time in return for instruction.

boycott—To refuse to buy or sell goods from a specific person, store, organization, or country.

charter—A written grant of rights made by a government or ruler to an individual.

compromise—A settlement in which each side gives up some of its demands.

inoculate—To give medication in order to prevent a serious disease.

letter of credit—A letter giving permission for the holder to withdraw money from another person's account.

levy—To vote approval to collect taxes.

negotiate—To discuss and bargain until an agreement is reached.

prevail—To be stronger or more important.

Privy Council—Advisors to Great Britain's king.

proprietor—A person who legally owns property.

shilling—A coin used in colonial America.

smallpox—An infectious disease that causes vomiting, fevers, and open sores on the skin.

tallow—A substance used in making candles.

Further Reading

Books

Collier, Christopher, and James Lincoln Collier. *Creating the Constitution: 1787*. Tarrytown, N.Y.: Marshall Cavendish Corporation, 1998.

Cousins, Margaret. *Ben Franklin of Old Philadelphia*. New York: Random House Children's Books, 2004

Ferrie, Richard. *The World Turned Upside Down: George Washington and the Battle of Yorktown*. New York: Holiday House, Inc., 1998.

Fingeroth, Danny. *Democracy's Signature: Benjamin Franklin and the Declaration of Independence*. New York: The Rosen Publishing Group, Inc., 2003.

Hull, Mary E. *The Boston Tea Party in American History.* Berkeley Heights, N.J.: Enslow Publishers, 1999.

Leebrick, Kristal. *The Constitution*. Mankato, Minn.: Capstone Press, Inc., 2002.

Internet Addresses

Ben's Guide to U.S. Government for Kids, Grades 6–8. May 4, 2001. <http://bensguide.gpo.gov/6-8/index.html>.

Jump Back in Time: Revolutionary Period (1764–1789). "America's Story from America's Library." *The Library of Congress*. n.d. <http://www.americaslibrary.gov/cgi-bin/page.cgi/jb/revolut>.

Revolutionary War. "American History." *About, Inc.* © 2002. <http://americanhistory.about.com/cs/revolutionarywar/>.

Places to Visit

Benjamin Franklin's Grave
Christ Church Cemetery
Fifth and Arch Streets
Philadelphia, PA 19106

Benjamin Franklin House
36 Craven Street
London, England
44-020-7930-9121
http://www.rsa.org.uk/franklin/fbfh/default.html

Fireman's Hall
147 North Second Street
Philadelphia, PA 19106
(215) 923-1438

Independence National Historical Park
313 Walnut Street
Philadelphia, PA 19106
(215) 597-8974

International Printing Museum
315 East Torrance Boulevard
Carson, CA 90745
http://www.printmuseum.org

Index